THE MIGHTY PRINCE

Merlin L. Neff

Pacific Press® Publishing Association
Nampa, Idaho
Oshawa, Ontario, Canada
www.pacificpress.com

Cover design by Gerald Lee Monks
Cover illustration by Clyde Provonsha
Inside design by Steve Lanto

All Scriptures quoted are from The New King James Version, copyright © 1979, 1980, 1982, Thomas Nelson, Inc., Publishers.

Library of Congress Cataloging-in-Publication Data

Neff, Merlin L.
The mighty Prince / Merlin L. Neff.
p. cm.— (Champions of faith ; v. 4)
ISBN 13: 978-0-8163-2267-1 (hard cover)
ISBN 10: 0-8163-2267-8 (hard cover)
1. Jesus Christ—Biography—Juvenile literature. I. Title.
BT302.N357 2008
232.9'01—dc22

2008008080

Additional copies of this book are available by calling toll-free
1-800-765-6955 or by visiting http://www.adventistbookcenter.com.

08 09 10 11 12 • 5 4 3 2 1

"Train up a child in the way he should go, and when he is old he will not depart from it."

—Proverbs 22:6

Interior Illustrations:

Harry Anderson: pages 20, 25, 56, 57, 80, 92, 149.
Robert Ayres: pages 77, 81.
Ken Gunall: page 144.
Lars Justinen: pages 69, 133.
Joe Maniscalco: pages 8, 36, 37, 120, 124, 128, 152, 156.
Clyde Provonsha: pages 1, 13, 24, 112, 113.
John Steel: pages 16, 17, 29, 33, 40, 44, 45, 49, 52, 60, 64, 68, 74, 84, 88, 96, 100, 104, 109, 116, 141, 148, 160.
Helen Torrey: page 72.
Charles Zingaro: pages 137, 145.

CONTENTS

Chapter 1   An Angel's Promise to a Priest 9

Chapter 2   Shepherds Hear the Angels Sing 13

Chapter 3   Wise Men Come to Worship the Prince 19

Chapter 4   Growing Up in Nazareth 23

Chapter 5   After Victory Comes Temptation 28

Chapter 6   The Men Who Followed Jesus 34

Chapter 7   Crowds Come to Hear Jesus 43

Chapter 8   Healing the Sick and the Dying 49

Chapter 9   How Jesus Kept the Sabbath 54

Chapter 10   The Courage of John the Baptist 61

Chapter 11   Jesus Goes to a Feast 66

Chapter 12   A Stormy Sea and Two Madmen 73

Chapter 13   Jesus and a Girl and a Boy 77

Chapter 14   A Vision of Glory 83

Chapter 15   Loving God and Helping Our Neighbors 89

Chapter 16   Learning to Love 98

Chapter 17   At the Grave of Lazarus 105

Chapter 18   Zacchaeus Up a Tree 109

Chapter 19   Jesus Meets Enemies and Friends 115

Chapter 20   The Lord's Supper 121

Chapter 21   Betrayed With a Kiss 126

Chapter 22   Jesus a Prisoner 130

Chapter 23   The King of the Jews 136

Chapter 24   Nailed to a Cross 142

Chapter 25   The Empty Tomb 149

Chapter 26   "I Am With You Always" 155

FOR PARENTS

**Pass Your Values On to Your Children
Through Bible Stories**

As a parent, you likely want your nine- or ten- or eleven-year-old daughter or son to enter the teen years knowing the most important stories of the Bible. As you look for ways to pass on to your child the love of God and the principles that represent His character, consider how well a good story captures the attention of human beings of all ages. The Bible stories in these five volumes will place God's principles in your child's mind in such a way that they won't forget them as they grow older.

Read these books with your child—or have the child read the story to you—morning or evening or Sabbath afternoon, every week. This is a good way to build your child's character and faith in God without your having to explain a bunch of abstract ideas. Their awareness of how God works with His people will grow without them realizing it.

Every generation through history that forgot about the Scriptures, and therefore the knowledge and implementation of God's principles, has suffered greatly from its own evil and self-destructive actions. A similar destiny awaits the children of this generation if we fail to bring the stories of the Bible to bear on their lives. The stakes are too high, the dangers too close, for us to neglect the story of salvation as we raise our children.

The timeless truths of the Bible come through clearly in the stories of this five-volume set. Each story has been screened for some elements more suited to adult readers. The stories chosen are the ones that follow the thread of salvation down through the centuries. In places where people of the Bible speak to each other, the words are quoted from the New King James Version, which is fairly easy to understand and widely accepted.

Pray for your child that he or she will respond positively when the Holy Spirit speaks to his or her heart. These Bible stories may bring your child to a turning point of knowing God in their own experience and accepting His love and His principles for themselves. There is supernatural power in the Word of God that may change your son or daughter forever.

The Publisher

AN ANGEL'S PROMISE TO A PRIEST

Luke 1

W hen kings and princes traveled in the early days of Israel, it had been the custom to send men to run ahead of them to prepare the way. If the king rode in a chariot, men would go far before him, removing rocks and smoothing the rough places in the road. Other men would shout, "The king is coming!" When Joseph was made a ruler in Egypt, servants went before him, commanding the people to bow to the king's highest officer. When Ahab hurried to his palace to escape a fierce storm, Elijah ran ahead to show him the way.

Prophets of Israel had declared that a man would come to prepare the way for the Messiah just as men prepared the way for a king. Six hundred years before the Savior came, Isaiah described a prophet who would appear and announce the coming Prince of Peace. He would be "the voice of one crying in the wilderness: 'Prepare the way of the Lord.' " Who was this advance guard? What message did he bring to the waiting Jewish nation?

A very old man of Israel, Zacharias, lived with his wife, Elizabeth, in the hill country of Judea. At that time, Herod was king of Judea. Zacharias was a priest, and at special times of the year, he and hundreds of other priests went to Jerusalem to burn incense on the altar in the temple and to carry out other sacred duties.

On one occasion, while Zacharias was offering incense in the temple, an angel appeared to him, standing at the right side of the altar. This was a good sign. Nevertheless, Zacharias was startled and fearful. The angel said, "Do not be afraid, Zacharias, for your prayer is heard; and your wife Elizabeth will bear you a son, and you shall call his name John. And you will have joy and gladness, and many will rejoice at his birth. For he will be great in the sight of the Lord, and shall drink neither wine nor strong drink. He will also be filled with the Holy Spirit, even from his mother's womb. And he will turn many of the children of Israel to the Lord their God."

GOD SAYS:
" 'For with God nothing will be impossible.' " –Luke 1:37

Now, Zacharias and his wife had longed for children for many years. But their wish had never been granted. The good news that they were to have a son was more than the old priest could believe. The angel saw that Zacharias doubted, so he told him, "I am Gabriel, who stands in the presence of God, and was sent to speak to you and bring you these glad tidings. But behold, you will be mute and not be able to speak until the day these things take place, because you did not believe my words which will be fulfilled in their own time."

The angel vanished, and the amazed Zacharias hurried out to bless the worshipers who were waiting and praying in the temple. When the pale-faced priest stood before them, however, he couldn't speak—not even a single word. He raised his hands over the people in a silent blessing. Everyone wondered what had happened and why Zacharias couldn't talk.

Elizabeth had a cousin named Mary, who lived in the town of Nazareth. The same glorious angel, Gabriel, who had visited Zacharias in the temple, came to Mary in Nazareth and said, "The Lord is with you; blessed are you among women!"

Mary was very surprised to see an angel, and she wondered what his words meant. So Gabriel spoke to her kindly and said, "Do not be afraid, Mary, for you have found favor with God. And behold, you will conceive in your womb and bring forth a Son, and shall call his name Jesus. He will be great, and will be called the Son of the Highest."

The angel also told Mary that her cousin Elizabeth was going to have a son too. When the heavenly messenger had finished speaking, Mary accepted his words, saying, "Let it be to me according to your word." Then Gabriel left her.

Every girl in Israel hoped that she might become the mother of the Messiah, the Savior of God's people. After Mary received the wonderful message that she would have a son and that he would be the Messiah, she went to visit her cousin Elizabeth, and the two women talked together about the promises the angel had made to them. Mary stayed at Elizabeth's home for about three months.

After a time, a son was born to Elizabeth and Zacharias just as the angel had said. Their relatives and neighbors rejoiced with the parents. They suggested that the boy should be named Zacharias after his father, but Elizabeth insisted that the baby would be named John. And Zacharias, who was still

QUICK FACT:

Because Zacharias showed doubt, he was unable to speak until the angel's words came true.

11

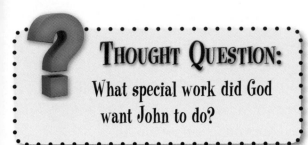

THOUGHT QUESTION:

What special work did God want John to do?

unable to speak, wrote on a tablet, "His name is John." Everyone there was amazed, because at that moment Zacharias was able to talk again. He told the friends and relatives what the angel had said to him in the temple. Then he blessed his son, saying,

> "And you, child, will be called the prophet of the Highest;
> For you will go before the face of the Lord to prepare His ways,
> To give knowledge of salvation to His people
> By the remission of their sins" (Luke 1:76, 77).

John grew to become a strong, good boy. He was the one God chose to be "the voice." He was the one who would go before the Messiah to prepare the way for Him.

SHEPHERDS HEAR THE ANGELS SING

Luke 2:1–38

The sun had set over the hills near Bethlehem, the city of David. Shepherds were guarding their flocks of sheep. Lions and jackals sneaked out of their caves, looking for food. Hungry hyenas and wolves prowled in the darkness, and sometimes robbers tried to slip in and steal the sheep. So it was necessary for the shepherds to stand guard in the darkness and protect their flocks from danger.

On this chilly night, the shepherds were watching their sheep in the fields. The lonely hours were broken only by the occasional howl of a jackal or the cry of a night bird. Suddenly, a glorious light flashed from the sky, shining down all around them.

Startled and afraid, the men hid their faces and cried out in fear. When their eyes became accustomed to the brightness, the shepherds saw an angel standing before them, and they heard him say, "Do not be afraid, for behold, I bring you good tidings of great joy which will be to all people. For there is born to you this day in the city of David a Savior, who is Christ the Lord."

GOD SAYS:

" 'For there is born to you this day in the city of David a Savior, who is Christ the Lord.' " –Luke 2:11

As these humble men listened to the angel, glorious pictures filled their minds. Truly, the angel's message was "good tidings of great joy." For a long time, they had been waiting and hoping for the Messiah to come and save them from the power of Rome. And now He had come at last! He was in Bethlehem, their hometown, only a little distance away! Where would they find the King? What would He look like?

The angel continued speaking. "And this will be the sign to you: You will find a Babe wrapped in swaddling cloths, lying in a manger." Then the heavenly messenger was joined by a whole chorus of shining angels. Like a vast army, they moved above the hills and plains; in their light, the fields and plains could be seen as clearly as in the noonday sun.

The shepherds stood silent, frozen in their tracks, listening. Then they heard the sweetest music they had ever heard in all their lives. It was a song of heaven:

"Glory to God in the highest,
And on earth peace, goodwill toward men!"
(Luke 2:14).

Gradually the light faded as the angels moved across the sky, and once more shadows surrounded the shepherds and their flocks. They paid no attention to the darkness, however, because a bright hope burned in their hearts. "Glory to God in the highest!" they sang.

"Let us now go to Bethlehem and see this thing that has come to pass, which the Lord has made known to us," they said to one another. So, running and stumbling along the rocky trail, they came at last to the Bethlehem road. As they hurried along the highway, they must have whispered excitedly, wondering why the Messiah would be lying in a manger—when He was a royal Prince.

Here is how it came about. The emperor of Rome had ordered all the people in the empire to go to their hometowns to register and be counted, so that all the taxes could

? THOUGHT QUESTION: Why did God choose shepherds to be the first to welcome the Son of God into the world?

be collected accurately. Since Mary traced her family line through the descendants of David, she and Joseph had to register at Bethlehem. This was the town where David had been born, and on the surrounding hills, he had guarded his father's flocks.

So, Mary and her carpenter husband, Joseph, had to travel from Nazareth to Bethlehem. On the way they must have passed through the towns of Shiloh and Gilgal, and they may have stopped in Jerusalem.

Joseph and Mary were poor. When they came to the little town of Bethlehem, they found it filled with visitors. They tried to find a place to stay for the night, but there was no room for them at the inn. After searching everywhere for a resting place, Joseph at last found shelter in one of the cattle sheds. There

Mary lay down to rest, and there her Son, Jesus, was born.

The shepherds hurried through the dark streets of Bethlehem, searching for the Christ child. At last, seeing a flicker of light, they entered the shed and found Joseph standing guard by a manger. In the shadows were cows, oxen, and donkeys, and as the visitors drew nearer they caught a glimpse of a young woman lying on the straw. Near Mary, in the manger—the food box for the cattle—was her newborn Son, wrapped in tight bands of linen cloth, called "swaddling cloth."

From these shepherds, Joseph and Mary heard the wonderful news of how the angels had announced the Messiah's birth. They heard how the angel choir sang above the Bethlehem hills. Perhaps a shepherd boy sang the chorus softly while Baby Jesus slept.

"Glory to God in the highest,
And on earth peace, goodwill toward men!"
(Luke 2:14).

Soon the shepherds said Goodbye to Mary and Joseph and left. Before long, the sleepy little town stirred, awoke, and then became excited over the news. Soon everyone had heard the shepherds' story and began to wonder about the strange event; but in the cattle shed Mary treasured every word the shepherds had spoken. Later, she thought of these words again and again during days of disappointment and sorrow.

The shepherds returned to

their flocks of sheep, thanking God for the wonderful message they had received. "Glory to God in the highest" kept ringing in their ears, and their hearts were glad because they had seen the Christ child.

These humble shepherds of the hills were the only ones to hear the glorious song of the angels. They were the first visitors to set eyes on the

Mighty Prince who would save His people from their sins.

About six weeks after Jesus was born, Joseph and Mary traveled the six miles from Bethlehem to Jerusalem to present the Baby Jesus at the temple and to make an offering to the Lord according to the laws written in the scrolls. A lamb should be offered for a burnt offering and a pigeon or dove for a sin offering. But if the parents were poor and couldn't afford this offering, they could bring two turtledoves to the temple.

QUICK FACT:
Simeon and Anna knew who Baby Jesus was because God revealed it to them.

Joseph guided Mary through the crowds as she tenderly carried her baby in her arms. Money changers were shouting in the temple court, and traders were selling sheep, oxen, and doves for sacrifices. The bewildered couple seemed lost in the busy throng. When the priest finally accepted their offering of the doves and blessed the Child, he did not realize what a special day this was. As he wrote the name *Jesus* on the records, he did not recognize that this Child was the promised Messiah.

About this time, Simeon, a good man who lived in Jerusalem, came into the temple. For years he had prayed for the coming of the Messiah, and God's Spirit had assured him that he would not die before he had seen the Christ. As Simeon saw Mary holding Baby Jesus, he realized that this was the promised Savior. He spoke to Joseph and Mary and held the Child in his arms. Simeon thanked God and began to pray.

While Simeon was speaking, an aged prophetess named Anna came into the temple, and she, too, recognized that this Baby was the long-awaited Messiah. She praised God for His blessings and told all her friends in Jerusalem that the Savior of Israel had come.

WISE MEN COME TO WORSHIP THE PRINCE

Matthew 2

T he shepherds at Bethlehem were not the only ones to see glorious signs in the heavens announcing the Messiah's coming. In a land far to the east lived wise men, or Magi, who studied the stars. They knew the promises in the Old Testament concerning the coming Messiah, the Son of God.

One night as they were scanning the heavens, they saw an unusual new star in the west. They decided that this bright star must be the sign of the Messiah, the King of the Jews, and they repeated the ancient prophecy of Balaam in the Old Testament:

> "A Star shall come out of Jacob;
> A Scepter shall rise out of Israel" (Numbers 24:17).

The wise men loaded a camel caravan with precious gifts and soon set out on the long journey across the desert to Jerusalem. Each night, they saw the star ahead of them, and it guided and cheered them on their way.

When the Magi arrived at the gates of Jerusalem, they questioned the city guards, asking, "Where is He who has been born King of the Jews? For we have seen His star in the East and have

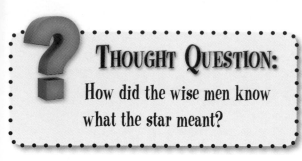

THOUGHT QUESTION:

How did the wise men know what the star meant?

come to worship Him."

Strangely enough, no one in the city seemed to know what these strangers were talking about! The priests who carried out the temple services were not ready to welcome the Messiah. The men in the market were too busy thinking of money to make room in their lives for the Christ.

However, news of the wise men's search soon reached the ears of King Herod. Anxious to find the basis for the rumor about the birth of a king, Herod gathered the priests and scribes before him and demanded to know where the Messiah was to be born.

The leaders of Israel replied, "In Bethlehem of Judea, for thus it is written by the prophet:

> 'But you, Bethlehem, in the land of Judah,
> Are not the least among the rulers of Judah;
> For out of you shall come a Ruler
> Who will shepherd My people Israel' "
>
> (Matthew 2:6, 7).

When crafty King Herod heard this, he called the wise men to his court and in a friendly manner urged them to continue their search for the Christ child. He said, "Go and search carefully for the young Child, and when you have found Him, bring back word to me, that I may come and worship Him also." The king seemed eager for the Magi to go to Bethlehem and search for the new heir to Israel's throne.

Once more the wise men set out on their journey. Once more they saw the star, and this time it led them to Bethlehem. The star guided the wise men to the humble place where Joseph and Mary were living with Baby Jesus.

When the men of the East entered the house and saw the Child with His mother, they bowed before Him and acknowledged Him as their Lord. Then they opened their treasure boxes and gave the young Prince expensive presents—frankincense (a costly ointment and perfume), myrrh (a rich, spicy sap from thorn trees), and gold.

How Mary must have marveled that these wealthy scholars from the East would travel to Bethlehem to worship the Christ child! The wise men had strong faith to believe that Jesus was the Son of God!

> **QUICK FACT:**
> It was the custom to offer gifts to princes as a show of respect, which is why the wise men brought Jesus the richest gifts they could afford.

After they found Jesus, the wise men were warned in a dream not to report their discovery to King Herod. Instead, they set out at once on their homeward journey, but they went by a different route so that they did not pass through Jerusalem.

That same night, after the Magi had gone, Joseph also received a warning dream. An angel told him, "Arise, take the young Child and His mother, flee to Egypt, and stay there until I bring you word; for Herod will seek the young Child to destroy Him."

Joseph awakened Mary and told her of the danger. Without waiting for daylight, they began the long trip to Egypt. Every hour of the day they feared that Herod's soldiers might overtake them. They were safe, however, angels from heaven were guarding the little Prince.

Joseph and Mary arrived in the strange country of Egypt. They were poor, but the rich gifts the wise men had given to Jesus helped supply their needs in this time of danger.

Back in Bethlehem, death struck soon after Joseph and Mary left. When the wise men did not return to King Herod's court, the proud monarch realized he had been tricked. In an insane fury, he issued a terrible decree, ordering his soldiers to go to Bethlehem and kill every boy two years old or younger. The Roman soldiers marched into the town and slaughtered the innocent children, and Herod was satisfied. He believed he had gotten rid of the Baby who might threaten his throne.

GOD SAYS:

"They saw the young Child with Mary His mother, and fell down and worshiped Him." –Matthew 2:11

Later, after King Herod had died, the angel of the Lord appeared again to Joseph in Egypt and told him, "Arise, take the young Child and His mother, and go to the land of Israel, for those who sought the young Child's life are dead."

The family decided to return to their former home in Nazareth, and the words of the prophet, written long before Jesus was born, were now fulfilled. The prophecy had said, "He shall be called a Nazarene."

GROWING UP IN NAZARETH

Luke 2:40–52

One day, as Joseph and Mary journeyed back to their homeland from Egypt, they grew excited. They began to recognize certain things in the countryside, and the road was becoming more and more familiar. Yes, they were almost home!

Joseph urged the donkey forward as they climbed the winding road that led by the Hill of Precipitation, a familiar landmark to the people of Nazareth. A chubby little Boy Jesus ran alongside His mother, Mary. He was wide-eyed with excitement, because everything He saw was new to Him. When the travelers reached the top of the hill, they stopped and looked down on the town of Nazareth nestled in the hollows below. Here and there, olive groves dotted the slopes, and six miles to the west lay the blue Sea of Galilee.

As Joseph and Mary entered the narrow, crooked streets of the town, friends welcomed them. They paid special attention to the Boy Jesus, who had been born after Mary left Nazareth.

Yes, it was good to be home again. Joseph had not dreamed, when they went to Bethlehem, that they would be away so long. As soon as the family was settled in a small cottage, the carpenter opened his shop for business. No doubt he worked long hours, making tables and stools, wooden bowls and kneading troughs, plow handles and ox yokes.

When the Boy Jesus was old enough to help, He worked in the carpenter shop with Joseph. Jesus must have been a careful worker with the hammer and saw. He knew how to make a wooden yoke for a pair of oxen. Later He talked about an "easy" yoke—one that would not injure the necks of the animals.

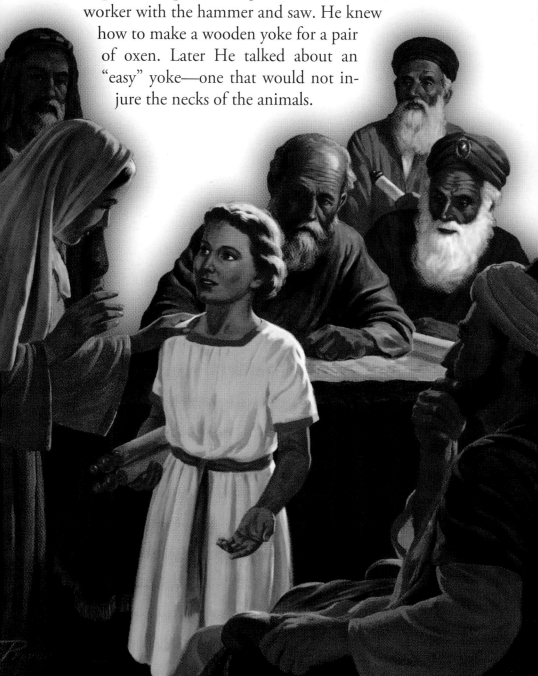

Jesus loved being outdoors. When He climbed up the side of Mount Tabor, He watched foxes slink into their holes in the rocks, and He saw the birds build their nests among the branches of oak trees. As a boy, it was probably His duty to care for the chickens, and many times He must have seen the mother hens gather their chicks under their wings. The Boy also knew the work of shepherds, and He probably helped them search for lost sheep.

Jesus saw the Roman soldiers. He saw them beat His people when they were disobedient. Sometimes prisoners were put to death by being crucified. This meant that the victims were stretched out on wooden crosses and their hands and feet were nailed to the beams. Then the crosses were lifted upright, and these unfortunate persons were left there to suffer until they died. The sight of such torture must have hurt Jesus very much, and He must have gone to His mother to ask what it all meant.

When He was young, Jesus learned to read. It was very important that every Jewish boy should know how to read the Old Testament writings. Jesus studied the books of Moses that told the history of His people. He loved the stories of the children of Israel escaping from Egypt and the glory of Israel during the reigns of King David and King Solomon. Jesus was familiar with the words of Isaiah, Jeremiah, and the other prophets, and He memorized many of the beautiful Psalms. He treasured God's law in His heart, because He knew the story of how God, on Mount Sinai, had given the Ten Commandments to the people. Jesus learned about the Feast of the Passover and how it was first observed on the night the children of Israel left Egypt. He knew, too, why a lamb was killed in every home on that occasion.

Like all devout Jews, Joseph and Mary went to the Passover Feast at the temple in Jerusalem each year. And when Jesus was twelve years old—the age at which boys were expected to start attending the feast—His parents took Him with them. It was springtime, and as the crowds of people traveled to Jerusalem, they sang and played musical instruments and enjoyed the trip.

The Boy Jesus was thrilled to see the capital city for the first time. As He entered the temple courts, He could see in the distance the great altar where the priests offered sacrifices. He knew the meaning of the sacrifice and how they represented the Lamb of God who would die for the sins of the world.

QUICK FACT:
As a child Jesus carefully studied God's word and spent time in nature.

In one area of the temple, learned rabbis sat, teaching their pupils. Jesus was interested in what these teachers were saying, and He slipped away from His mother and went to where the rabbis were gathered. He sat down to listen and to ask questions.

When the Passover Feast had ended, Joseph and Mary started home. Although Jesus wasn't with them, they didn't worry. They had many friends in the crowd who were traveling back to Nazareth, and they thought Jesus was with some of them.

When night came, however, and they couldn't find Jesus, Mary became worried. She and Joseph searched through the crowd, but no one had seen the Boy. Joseph and Mary returned to Jerusalem in a hurry. They searched in all the places they had stayed, but the boy was not there.

THOUGHT QUESTION: What did Jesus mean when He said, "I must be about My Father's business"?

Finally, on the third day they went to the temple, and there they found Jesus among the teachers, listening and asking questions. Everyone who heard the twelve-year-old Boy was astonished at the answers He gave. When Joseph and Mary saw Him, they were amazed, and Mary said, "Son, why have You done this to us? Look, Your father and I have sought You anxiously."

The Boy Jesus answered, "Why did you seek Me? Did you not know that I must be about My Father's business?"

Mary hardly knew what to say. But then Jesus left the teachers and returned with Joseph and Mary to Nazareth.

As the years passed in Nazareth, Jesus continued to work and study. He grew older and "increased in wisdom and stature, and in favor with God and men."

AFTER VICTORY COMES TEMPTATION

Matthew 3:1–4:12; Luke 3:2–22; John 1

Excitement spread quickly through Nazareth. People were gathered in little groups. They were talking about the new prophet who was preaching down by the Jordan River. He was telling the people that God's kingdom was near. Some believed that this new prophet was Elijah who had come down from heaven; others declared that he was the promised Messiah.

Jesus listened to the people talking. He was now thirty years old. As He listened, He soon learned that this new prophet was his cousin John—the son who had been born to Zacharias and Elizabeth about the same time that Jesus had been born.

John had been living for years in the desert. He had never cut his hair or shaved. He ate simple food and drank no wine; his clothing was a coarse coat of camel's hair held in place by a leather belt.

Soldiers, priests, country people, and men from Jerusalem went out to the Jordan River to hear John preach. They heard him say he was

" 'The voice of one crying in the wilderness:
"Make straight the way of the Lord," ' "

as the prophet Isaiah said" (John 1:23). John told the people to live right and to obey God. "Bear fruits worthy of repentance," he declared.

"What shall we do then?" the people asked him.

"He who has two tunics," John answered, "let him give to him who has none; and he who has food, let him do likewise." He warned the tax collectors not to cheat or be dishonest, and he called upon the soldiers to be kind to the people. Many who heard the prophet repented of their sins and were baptized in the Jordan River.

One day Jesus left the carpenter shop at Nazareth and went to Bethabara, about thirty miles away, to hear John preach. When Jesus came near, the prophet saw Him and said to the people, "Behold! The Lamb of God who takes away the sin of the world! This is He of whom I said, 'After me comes a Man who is preferred before me, for He was before me.' "

John knew that angels had announced Jesus' birth in Bethlehem. He had received news of Jesus as Mary's Son grew up in Nazareth—a good, kind, and sinless young man. When Jesus came to hear John preach at the Jordan River, He asked John to baptize Him. But the prophet said, "I need to be baptized by You, and are You coming to me?"

GOD SAYS:
"Now Jesus Himself began His ministry at about thirty years of age."
-Luke 3:23

Jesus answered, "Permit it to be so now, for thus it is fitting for us to fulfill all righteousness." So John baptized Jesus.

Jesus did not need to be baptized, because He had done nothing wrong. But He was baptized as an example to us—an example that we should follow. We show our love and loyalty to our heavenly Father when we turn away from our sins and are baptized.

When Jesus came up out of the water, the heavens opened. He saw the Spirit of God come down like a dove and land upon Him. A voice from heaven said, "This is My beloved Son, in whom I am well pleased."

Jesus knew it was time for Him to start the special work He had come to this earth to do. He left the crowds at the river and went up the steep trail into the wilderness—wild, rocky country where savage predators prowled. In the desert, He was alone to think and to plan how He would help human beings. He remembered the words He had heard from His Father in heaven: "This is My beloved Son, in whom I am well pleased."

Days and weeks passed, and still Jesus remained alone in the desert. How should He reach the people? How could He tell them about His Father's wonderful love for every man, woman, and child? Jesus knew that He had come to fight Satan, the enemy of God and man, and He realized that the struggle would be long and fierce.

For forty days Jesus fasted and prayed and planned His work. He became weak and hungry, tired and worn out. Suddenly the devil came to Him and said, "If You are the Son of God, command that these stones become bread."

Jesus was nearly starved with hunger. Surely if He were God's Son, He could make bread from the round stones lying on the ground. But Jesus never performed a miracle for Himself or His own benefit. Without hesitation, Christ shot these words at the enemy: "It is written, 'Man shall not live by bread alone, but by every word that proceeds from the mouth of God.'"

Jesus meant that there is something more important than food or clothing, houses or cars—God and his love are more important than all these things. In this hour of temptation, Jesus taught us that our first and greatest duty is to live by the words of our heavenly Father, even as He did.

When Satan couldn't defeat Christ by appealing to His appetite, he took Jesus to the highest dome on the temple at Jerusalem. Jesus had visited the temple many times, and He knew that people expected the Messiah to

QUICK FACT:
Jesus didn't need to be baptized-He had never sinned-but He wanted to be a good example for us.

appear there. Why should He not jump down into the courtyard so that the people would believe that He had come from heaven like an angel?

In that moment the tempter said, "If You are the Son of God, throw Yourself down. For it is written:

'He shall give His angels charge over you,'

and,

'In their hands they shall bear you up,
Lest you dash your foot against a stone' "
(Matthew 4:6).

Jesus shook His head. He knew that human beings must have faith in God's Word and in His promises. Jesus could not win people to Him by mere power or outward display. Therefore the Son of God quickly replied to Satan, "It is written again, 'You shall not tempt the Lord your God.' " Once more Jesus rebuffed the sly temptation of His enemy.

THOUGHT QUESTION:

Why did Jesus always answer Satan by quoting Scripture?

Then Satan took Jesus to the top of a high mountain and showed Him the nations of earth with their great cities, vast armies, palaces, riches, and glory. Surely Jesus had come to save the world. Was it not all lying here before Him, awaiting His rule? Satan whispered, "All these things I will give You if You will fall down and worship me."

The Son of God knew He could never save sinful, lost people in this way. He must suffer and die so that the world would be free from sin. With all His remaining strength, Jesus turned to His enemy and said, "Away with you, Satan! For it is writ-ten, 'You shall worship the Lord your God, and Him only you shall serve.' "

In every temptation Jesus quoted from the Holy Scriptures, and Satan could not stand against the truth. The enemy fled away, and Jesus felt at peace. He was exhausted by the struggle, but He was victorious. Angels came to Jesus, bringing Him food and ministering to His needs.

Soon the Son of God took the rough trail back to the Jordan River and then walked up the winding road to Galilee.

THE MEN WHO FOLLOWED JESUS

Matthew 4:17–25; Mark 1:14–38; Luke 4:31–41; 5:1–11; John 1:38–49; 2

Soon Jesus went from city to city in Galilee, saying, "The time is fulfilled, and the kingdom of God is at hand. Repent, and believe in the gospel." He preached in the synagogues, and the people listened to what He said, and some began to follow Him.

Jesus needed disciples who believed His message, men who would go and tell others the good news. Two men who had been listening to John the Baptist preach, came to talk to Jesus. When they came near, the Master said, "What do you seek?"

"Rabbi," they asked, "where are You staying?"

"Come and see," Jesus replied, inviting the men to follow Him.

Andrew and John, two fishermen from Bethsaida, followed Jesus and became His disciples. Andrew was a careful, cautious person, while young John was bold, energetic, and anxious to act. These men listened to Jesus, and later they heard John the Baptist declare that this Man from Nazareth was the Lamb of God, the Savior of the world. Andrew hurried to tell his brother, Simon Peter, about his astonishing discovery.

These men decided to follow Jesus wherever He went, trusting that He was the promised Messiah. Andrew never imagined that someday he would die for this newfound Friend. John did not guess that he would see visions of the new earth that Jesus is preparing for those who love Him.

The next day, as Jesus started walking to Galilee, He met Philip and asked him to be a disciple. Philip agreed and then hurried to tell his friend Nathanael what had happened.

"We have found Him of whom Moses in the law, and also the prophets, wrote," said Philip excitedly, "Jesus of Nazareth, the son of Joseph."

Nathanael looked doubtful. "Can anything good come out of Nazareth?" he asked.

"Come and see," urged Philip, and taking his friend by the arm, Philip led Nathanael to see Jesus.

Jesus saw Nathanael coming toward Him, and He said, "Behold, an Israelite indeed, in whom is no deceit!"

Nathanael still wasn't sure that Jesus was the Messiah, so he asked, "How do You know me?"

"Before Philip called you," Jesus answered, "when you were under the fig tree, I saw you."

Nathanael paused. Yes, he had been in a quiet grove of trees some distance away, praying for the Messiah to come! How could Jesus know that? From his heart the words came tumbling out, "Rabbi, You are the Son of God! You are the King of Israel!"

One day, while Jesus was walking by the Sea of Galilee, He saw Peter and Andrew and James and John standing in the water washing their fishing nets. Two fishing boats were anchored nearby, riding on the waves of the blue Galilee.

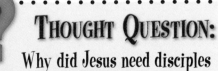

THOUGHT QUESTION: Why did Jesus need disciples for His ministry on earth?

"Launch out into the deep and let down your nets for a catch," suggested the Master.

Simon Peter was a fisherman with many years of experience. *What does a carpenter know about fishing?* Peter thought to himself. Anyone knew that the best time to catch fish was at night. The morning sun was already above the hills. Impulsively, Peter answered, "Master, we have toiled all night and caught nothing; nevertheless at Your word I will let down the net."

The fishermen went through the motions of spreading their nets and letting them down into the sea. Then they began to draw in the nets. Peter could not understand. The nets were heavy, loaded down with fish! There were so many fish the men couldn't lift the catch alone. They shouted for help, and another boat pulled alongside. Fish, fish everywhere! The boats were loaded to the gunwales and would have been swamped if the fishermen had not acted quickly and pulled them ashore.

Peter was amazed, and he was also quick

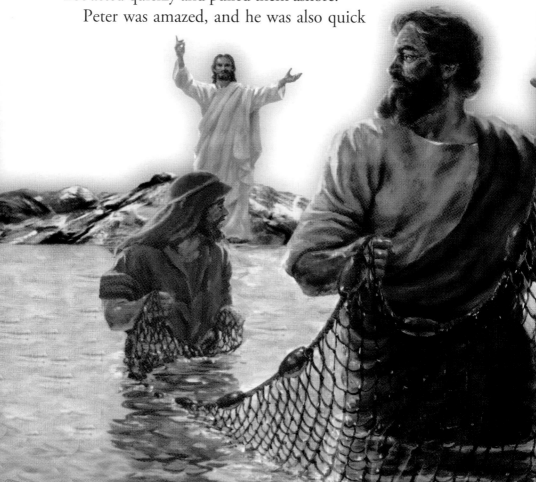

to admit his mistake. Falling down before Jesus, the fisherman said, "Depart from me, for I am a sinful man, O Lord!"

"Do not be afraid," Jesus answered. "From now on you will catch men." Then the four men—Andrew, Peter, James, and John—left their boats and their fishing and followed the Master as His disciples.

One by one, other men were drawn to Jesus as well. They left their regular work to follow the Teacher who thrilled the crowds. Soon the Master had twelve disciples to help Him in His ministry.

One evening Jesus and His disciples went to the little town of Cana, a few miles north of Nazareth, where there was great excitement. The people were milling about in the narrow streets, waiting for a wedding. Torches made the dark alleyways bright, and houses were decorated for the occasion. Soon the people could hear music and singing. The bride was on her way to the bridegroom's house.

GOD SAYS:

" 'Follow Me, and I will make you fishers of men.' " -Matthew 4:19

Among the guests invited to the wedding were Jesus and His disciples. Perhaps the bride or bridegroom was a relative of Mary, Jesus' mother, for she was helping with the wedding feast.

In the middle of the celebration the host was faced with an embarrassing situation. He discovered that there was no more wine for the guests. Mary came to her Son, Jesus, and said, "They have no wine."

"What does your concern have to do with Me?" Jesus asked His mother. "My hour has not yet come." He wasn't being disrespectful to His mother; He knew that if He performed a miracle the news would be broadcast through the land and thousands of curious people would flock to see Him for the wrong reason.

His mother had faith in her Son's power, however, and she said to the servants, "Whatever He says to you, do it."

There were six large waterpots standing nearly empty nearby. The water had been used to wash the hands and feet of the guests as they arrived. Jesus saw these waterpots, each large enough to hold twenty or thirty gallons, and He said to the servants, "Fill the waterpots with water."

The servants filled them to the brim. Then Jesus said to them, "Draw some out now, and take it to the master of the feast."

The servants were puzzled by this strange instruction, but they went ahead and dipped out of the big jars. Then they looked at one another in amazement. The water had become wine! When the master of the feast tasted this wine, he called the bridegroom and said to him, "Every man at the beginning sets out the good wine, and when the guests have well drunk, then the inferior. You have kept the good wine until now!"

This miracle of turning the water to wine caused Jesus' disciples to have greater faith in Him. The Son of God is the Creator of the world, and His miracles should not surprise us. Every year the dry, brown stalks of the grapevine become green and bear grapes, which have sweet juice in them. Only God's creative power can cause these vines to grow. The same miracle that Jesus performed in a moment of time—turning water into wine—He causes to take place in nature each year, as grapes grow and ripen.

QUICK FACT:
The turning of the water into wine was Jesus' first miracle.

After the miracle in Cana, Jesus traveled to Capernaum, a small town on the west side of the Sea of Galilee. On the Sabbath day, He went to the synagogue, the Jewish church, and the attendant invited Him to speak. The people were amazed at His words, because He spoke with authority.

A man in the synagogue was possessed by an evil spirit, and he screamed, "Let us alone! What have we to do with You, Jesus of Nazareth? Did You come to destroy us? I know who You are—the Holy One of God!"

Jesus turned and spoke boldly to the devil in the crazed man, "Be quiet, and come out of him!"

Then the demon threw the man down on the floor right in front of everyone in the synagogue and came out of the man without doing him any harm. Everyone was amazed, and they said to each other, "What a word this is! For with authority and power He commands the unclean spirits, and they come out."

When Jesus left the synagogue, He went home with Simon Peter, His disciple. Arriving at Peter's house, the Master found Simon's mother-in-law seriously ill with a fever. The family hoped that Jesus would help her. As the Master stood by the sick woman's bedside, He took her by the hand and lifted her up. Immediately, the fever left her, and she got out of bed and helped prepare dinner.

That evening after the sun went down and the Sabbath was over, the people of Capernaum brought their sick friends and relatives to Simon Peter's house. Jesus laid His hands on each sick person and cured him or her. The next morning, before daybreak, Jesus woke up and left the house and went to a lonely spot on a hillside, where He prayed.

Now it was almost time for the Passover Feast, so Jesus and His disciples left Capernaum and traveled to Jerusalem. This was the same feast that Jesus had first attended when He was twelve years old. No doubt, He had been to the temple many times since He was a boy, and each time He remembered that He must do His Father's business.

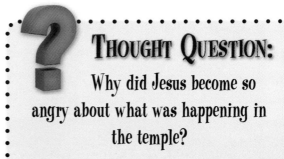

THOUGHT QUESTION:
Why did Jesus become so angry about what was happening in the temple?

Thousands of people came to Jerusalem each year to attend the feast. As usual, the traders were selling oxen, sheep, and doves for sacrifices. The money changers took the Roman coins marked with the image of Caesar and exchanged them for the coins of Israel—the only coins that could be used in the temple. These greedy men made a large profit from the people when they exchanged these coins.

The merchants had turned the beautiful, sacred temple court into a noisy marketplace. The shouting and confusion made it almost impossible for a person to realize that he was in God's house. Then, too, the traders cheated the people by demanding high prices for the animals they were selling to be offered as sacrifices.

In the midst of the bleating of sheep, the cooing of doves, and the shrill noise of the bargainers, Jesus stood alone. He saw the priests and rulers going about their sacred duties without paying any attention to the business being carried on right in the house of God.

Then the people began to watch Jesus. His face was filled with sorrow and anger as He made a whip out of a piece of rope. In a moment, He stepped forward and raised His strong arm, demanding silence. Then in ringing tones He said, "Take these things away! Do not make My Father's house a house of merchandise!"

Everyone made a rush for the gates. The tables where the money changers had stacked their coins fell over, and coins scattered in all directions on the marble pavement. Someone let the sheep and oxen loose, and they began running out of the temple court, while shouts of terror arose from the milling crowds of people.

Soon the religious leaders gathered around Jesus and His disciples. They asked Jesus, "What sign do You show to us, since You do these things?"

He answered, "Destroy this temple, and in three days I will raise it up."

> **GOD SAYS:**
>
> "'For My house shall be called a house of prayer for all nations.'"
> —Isaiah 56:7

The Jews responded sarcastically, "It has taken forty-six years to build this temple, and will You raise it up in three days?" They misunderstood what Jesus said. He was speaking about His body as the temple of God. Later, after Jesus had died and then came out of the tomb alive after three days, the disciples remembered how He had promised that He would be raised up in three days.

Hundred of years before all this, the prophet Malachi had said,

> "And The Lord, whom you seek,
> Will suddenly come to His temple" (Malachi 3:1).

This prophecy was fulfilled when Jesus came to live with us on earth. He knew that the temple was supposed to be a house of prayer, but the Jewish leaders had allowed it to become a market, a place of business where men cheated one another.

Remember that the church is where God meets with His people. When we come with reverence into His house of prayer, we receive the blessing of His love.

CROWDS COME TO HEAR JESUS

Matthew 5:1–12, 17, 44, 45; 6:1, 6, 9–30; 7:24–27

The Jewish leaders did not like Jesus, especially when they saw the crowds of people flocking to listen to Him. Now that Jesus was back in the cities of Galilee after His visit to Jerusalem, the crowds were larger than ever. Sometimes He preached in the synagogues, sometimes He taught by the seaside, and sometimes He found His way to a grassy meadow among the hills, where He sat and taught the people.

One of His wonderful messages, known as the Sermon on the Mount, has been written down in the Bible for us to read. In this sermon, Jesus told the people how to find happiness and how to do good. In simple language that everyone understood, He said,

> "Blessed are the poor in spirit,
>   For theirs is the kingdom of heaven.
> Blessed are those who mourn,
>   For they shall be comforted.
> Blessed are the meek,
>   For they shall inherit the earth.
> Blessed are those who hunger and thirst for
>   righteousness,

For they shall be filled.
Blessed are the merciful,
    For they shall obtain mercy.
Blessed are the pure in heart,
    For they shall see God.
Blessed are the peacemakers,
    For they shall be called sons of God.
Blessed are those who are persecuted for
    righteousness' sake,
       For theirs is the kingdom of heaven.

"Blessed are you when they revile and persecute you,

and say all kinds of evil against you falsely for My sake.

"Rejoice and be exceedingly glad, for great is your reward in heaven, for so they persecuted the prophets who were before you" (Matthew 5:1–12).

The people listened and were amazed. When they were beaten and mistreated by the Roman soldiers, they often did not return good for evil. But Jesus was telling them to be glad when they suffered for His sake, because they would receive a rich reward in heaven.

As Jesus looked at the people who had gathered around Him, He knew that they were worried about how to have enough money and food and clothing. They seemed more interested in these things than in finding the way of eternal life. So Jesus told them, "Do not lay up for yourselves treasures on earth, where moth and rust destroy and where thieves break in and steal. . . . For where your treasure is, there your heart will be also."

As the Master looked above Him and saw the birds sitting in the branches of the trees, He pointed to them and said to the people, "You cannot serve God and mammon. Therefore, I say to you, do not worry about your life, what you will eat or what you will drink; nor about your body, what you will put on. Is not life more than food and the body more than clothing? Look at the birds of the air, for they neither sow nor reap nor gather into barns; yet your heavenly Father feeds them. Are you not of more value than they?"

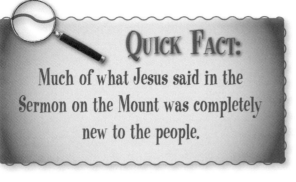

QUICK FACT:
Much of what Jesus said in the Sermon on the Mount was completely new to the people.

On the hillsides above Jesus, the spring wildflowers were growing. Perhaps some of the children had wandered off and were picking the blossoms. Jesus went on, "Why do you worry about clothing? Consider the lilies of the field, how they grow: they neither toil nor spin; and yet I say to you that even Solomon in all his glory was not arrayed like one of these. Now if God so clothes the grass of the field, which today is, and tomorrow is thrown into the oven, will He not much more clothe you, O you of little faith?"

When the Master spoke of love, the people listened carefully, for He was saying things they had never heard before. "I say to you," Jesus said, "love your enemies, bless those who curse you, do good to those who hate you, and pray for those who spitefully use you and persecute you, that you may be sons of your Father in heaven; for He makes His sun rise on the evil and on the good, and sends rain on the just and on the unjust.

For if you love those who love you, what reward have you?"

Jesus also warned against doing good things merely to show off before other people. He said, "Take heed that you do not do your charitable deeds before men, to be seen by them. Otherwise, you have no reward from your Father in heaven."

Jesus talked to the people about the Ten Commandments. He said, "Do not think that I came to destroy the Law or the Prophets. I did not come to destroy but to fulfill."

He urged the careless people in the crowd to listen to His words and to follow them. Jesus had been a carpenter, so He told the story of two men who had built houses. "Whoever hears these sayings of Mine and does them," He said, "I will liken him to a wise man who built his house on the rock: and the rain descended, the floods came, and the winds blew and beat on that house; and it did not fall, for it was founded on the rock. But everyone who hears these sayings of Mine, and does not do them, will be like a foolish man who built his house on the sand: and the rain descended, the floods came, and the winds blew and beat on that house; and it fell. And great was its fall."

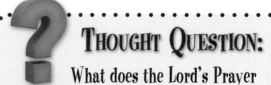

THOUGHT QUESTION:
What does the Lord's Prayer teach us about how to pray?

Jesus knew how to build houses, so He could give the best advice about foundations. He knew that every person must build his or her life upon the Rock of truth if the foundation is to be solid and strong.

At this time Jesus also taught His disciples how to pray. He said, "When you pray, go into your room, and when you have shut your door, pray to your Father who is in the secret place; and your Father who sees in secret will reward you openly." Then Jesus gave His disciples the wonderful model prayer we know as the Lord's Prayer. He said they should pray a prayer like this,

"Our Father in heaven,
Hallowed be Your name.
Your kingdom come.
Your will be done
On earth as it is in heaven.
Give us this day our daily bread.
And forgive us our debts,
As we forgive our debtors.
And do not lead us into temptation,
But deliver us from the evil one.
For Yours is the kingdom and the power and the glory for-
    ever. Amen" (Matthew 6:9–13).

When Jesus finished speaking, the large crowd of people was astonished at His words. He had told them to love their neighbors—yes, to love even their enemies! He had said they should be kind to the Roman soldiers who mistreated them and that they should seek God's kingdom more than anything else. When they looked at the birds, they remembered what Jesus had said about God's love; and when they saw the wild lilies growing in the field, they could not forget that Jesus had told them His Father loved them and would take care of them—just like He did the flowers.

GOD SAYS:
" 'For where your treasure is, there your heart will be also.' "
—Matthew 6:21

The Master's words stuck in the minds of the people who heard Him. And as they tried to do what He told them to do, they found new happiness in living.

HEALING THE SICK AND THE DYING

Matthew 8:1–13; Mark 2:1–12; Luke 7:11–16

Jesus traveled from town to town with His disciples. In some villages friends were waiting to welcome Him, because He had made them well when they were sick. However, some enemies among the Jews hated Jesus, and they scowled and whispered among themselves when He approached. The whole region of Galilee was stirred by the words and actions of the new Teacher, because the people knew that He taught with power and authority—unlike the Jewish scribes.

When Jesus entered the town of Capernaum, a Roman army captain came to Him, pleading for His help. The officer said, "Lord, my servant is lying at home paralyzed, dreadfully tormented."

Jesus answered, "I will come and heal him."

But the captain, being a humble man, answered, "Lord, I am not worthy that You should come under my roof. But only speak a word, and my servant will be healed."

When Jesus heard this, He was amazed and said to His disciples, "I say to you, I have not found such great faith, not even in Israel!" Then the Great Physician said to the captain, "Go your way; and as you have believed, so let it be done for you."

The captain believed the Master's words and hurried home. When he arrived, he found his servant was healed—just as Jesus had promised he would be.

Soon after this Jesus went to the town of Nain; His disciples and a crowd of people went with Him. As Jesus entered the

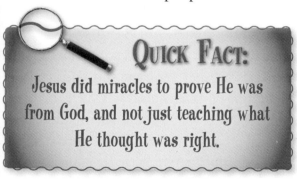

QUICK FACT:
Jesus did miracles to prove He was from God, and not just teaching what He thought was right.

gate of the village, He met a funeral procession coming out of the town on its way to the cemetery. The dead man was the only son of his widowed mother.

When Jesus saw the lonely, sorrowful woman, He pitied her and said to her, "Do not weep." Then the Master told the men who were carrying the body to stop. Speaking to the dead man, Jesus said, "Young man, I say to you, arise."

And the dead man did just that! He sat up and began to speak! Then Jesus took him to his mother, and she thanked God and cried for joy. When the people saw the miracle, they said, "A great prophet has risen up among us . . . God has visited His people."

In Jesus' time there were many lepers in Palestine. The terrible disease had no cure, and the men and women who were lepers couldn't live with their families and everyone else. They had to stay by themselves. It was the law that when the lepers went along the roads and streets, they had to cry out, "Unclean! Unclean!" so that healthy people could stay away from them.

As Jesus traveled along the road, a leper came to Him and fell on his knees before Jesus. He said, "Lord, if You are willing, You can make me clean."

Jesus stretched out His hand and touched the leper and said, "I am willing; be cleansed." And immediately the leprosy was cured. Then Jesus said to the man, "See that you tell no one; but go your way, show yourself to the priest, and offer the gift that Moses commanded."

The priests were also the physicians of the time. They were the only ones who could say whether a person was cured of a disease. So Jesus told the leper to go to the priest and have a physical examination before he mingled with the crowd.

One day Jesus was speaking to a group of people gathered in a house in Capernaum. A paralyzed man had heard that the Master was in town. He believed his disease would be cured if only he could be taken to the Savior. Four friends carried the paralyzed man on a stretcher to the place where Jesus was speaking, but with so many people crowded around the house, they couldn't get into the room where Jesus was. What were they to do?

One of the men who carried the stretcher thought of a plan. The four men took their sick friend up a stairway to the flat roof of the house. Then they began tearing off the tiles of the roof above the spot where Jesus was speaking!

When they had made the hole in the roof large enough, they gently lowered the stretcher, with the paralyzed man on it, through the hole they had made. Inside the house, the surprised crowd stepped back as they saw this

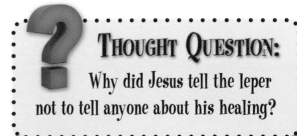

THOUGHT QUESTION:
Why did Jesus tell the leper not to tell anyone about his healing?

man coming down through the roof!

Jesus stopped speaking and looked too. He saw the faith this man had—faith to believe that Jesus could heal him. The Master said to the paralyzed man, "Son, your sins are forgiven you."

Some of Jesus' enemies were in the house listening, and they heard the Master say that the sick man's sins were forgiven. They began to whisper, "Why does this Man speak blasphemies like this? Who can forgive sins but God alone?"

Jesus saw the scowls on their jealous faces and heard their whispers. "Why do you reason about these things in your hearts?" He asked them. "Which is easier, to say to the paralytic, 'Your sins are forgiven you,' or to say, 'Arise, take up your bed and walk'? But that you may know that the Son of Man has power on earth to forgive sins"—

Quick Fact:
Jesus not only healed people's bodies; He healed their hearts and showed them God's love.

and at this point, Jesus turned to the paralyzed man who was lying on his stretcher and said, "I say to you, arise, take up your bed, and go to your house."

Immediately, the man was healed, and he got up, picked up his stretcher, and walked out of the house and headed toward his home! The people were amazed.

Jesus could forgive anyone's sins because He is the Son of God.

"We never saw anything like this!" the people said to each other as the paralyzed man left the house, shouting praises to God.

Jesus not only healed people, but He also taught them about His Father's love. He sympathized with them in their grief and comforted them in their sorrow. Wherever He went, He healed the sick. In some towns and villages, there was not one sick person left in the whole town after Jesus had been there; He had healed them all!

How wonderful it would be if Jesus were to come to our towns and cities today, healing the sick in the hospitals, raising the dead to life, making the blind to see and the deaf to hear!

The Master loved everyone, but many of the religious leaders hated Jesus and began to plot how they could stop His work.

How Jesus Kept the Sabbath

Luke 4:16–30; 6:1–12; John 5:1–14

Sunset on Friday evening marked the beginning of the holy Sabbath day, and none of the Jews did any work from that time until after sundown on Saturday night. The whole nation of Israel obeyed the fourth commandment, which declares, "Remember the Sabbath day, to keep it holy. Six days you shall labor, and do all your work, but the seventh day is the Sabbath of the Lord your God."

On the Sabbath day, the people went to the churches, which in the time of Jesus were called synagogues. It was the custom for the congregation to stand and face toward Jerusalem, where the temple was located. While standing, the people repeated these words: "Hear, O Israel: The Lord our God, the Lord is one! You shall love the Lord your God with all your heart, with all your soul, and with all your strength."

After the prayer was offered, the scrolls of the Old Testament were brought out, and a passage from the Scriptures was read. Then the teacher selected for the day, or someone chosen from the congregation, would talk to the people about the Scripture that had been read.

Jesus had not been in Nazareth for some time, but at last He returned to His hometown. On the Sabbath day, He went to the synagogue to worship, just as He always did on Sabbath. That Sabbath, Jesus was invited to read the Scripture in the synagogue service. The scroll of the prophet Isaiah was handed to Him, and He unrolled it and found the place where Isaiah prophesied about the Messiah who would come:

> "The Spirit of the Lord is upon Me,
> Because He has anointed Me
> To preach the gospel to the poor;
> He has sent Me to heal the brokenhearted,
> To proclaim liberty to the captives,
> And recovery of sight to the blind,
> To set at liberty those who are oppressed;
> To proclaim the acceptable year of the Lord"
> (Luke 4:18, 19).

When Jesus finished reading, He rolled up the scroll and gave it to the person in charge of the service. Then the carpenter's Son—Jesus the Messiah—sat down in the speaker's chair, and all the people watched Him, waiting to hear what He would say.

"Today this Scripture is fulfilled here in your hearing," Jesus said, beginning His sermon.

As Jesus continued preaching, the congregation was amazed at the gracious words that came from His lips. They began asking each other, "Is this not Joseph's son?" Some of these men and women had known Jesus for almost thirty years and were thrilled by His message. But others, who

GOD SAYS:

" 'The Sabbath was made for man, and not man for the Sabbath.' " –Mark 2:27

thought of Him only as a young man who had grown up in the town, scorned His words.

Jesus continued, "You will surely say this proverb to Me, 'Physician, heal yourself! Whatever we have heard done in Capernaum, do also here in Your country.' " Then He said, "Assuredly, I say to you, no prophet is accepted in his own country. But I tell you truly, many widows were in Israel in the days of Elijah, when the heaven was shut up three years and six months, and there was a great famine throughout all the land; but to none of them was Elijah sent except to Zarephath, in the region of Sidon, to a woman who was a widow. And many lepers were in Israel in the time of Elisha the prophet, and none of them was cleansed except Naaman the Syrian."

When the people heard this, they became angry with Jesus and began shouting. Some of them rushed at Jesus and dragged Him out of the synagogue and through the streets of Nazareth. They took Him to a high cliff where they planned to throw Him over so that He would be killed on the rocks below.

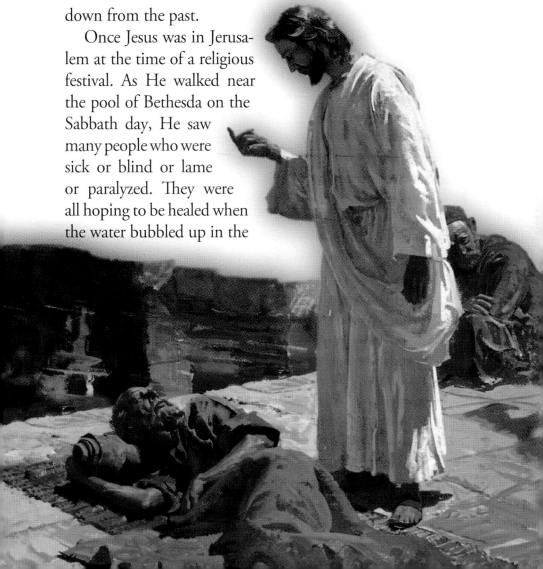

But in that moment, when Jesus was near death, angels from heaven protected the Son of God. He walked away from the mob, and not one person dared to lay a hand upon Him.

The Jewish leaders found fault with Jesus because He helped people and healed them on the Sabbath day. The Pharisees, a group of Jews who claimed to keep the law better than anyone else, had made many burdensome rules about what could be done on the Sabbath—and what could not be done. These rules were not God's rules; they were rules that men had made, traditions that had been handed down from the past.

Once Jesus was in Jerusalem at the time of a religious festival. As He walked near the pool of Bethesda on the Sabbath day, He saw many people who were sick or blind or lame or paralyzed. They were all hoping to be healed when the water bubbled up in the pool. The people believed that at certain times an angel stirred the water in the pool of Bethesda, and when that happened, whoever stepped into the pool first would be healed.

QUICK FACT:

The Jewish leaders didn't understand what the Sabbath was really about and made it into a day to be endured, not enjoyed.

The Master saw a helpless man lying near the pool. He had been sick for thirty-eight years. Jesus said to him, "Do you want to be made well?"

"Sir," the sick man replied, "I have no man to put me into the pool when the water is stirred up; but while I am coming, another steps down before me."

"Rise," Jesus commanded him with a loving smile, "take up your bed and walk."

The man's shrunken legs became strong immediately. He got up, picked up his mat, and walked! When the Jewish leaders saw this man carrying his mat on the Sabbath day, they said, "It is the Sabbath; it is not lawful for you to carry your bed."

"He who made me well said to me, 'Take up your bed and walk,' " answered the man who had been sick for so long.

"Who is the Man who said to you, 'Take up your bed and walk'?" asked the religious leaders. But the man who had been healed didn't know who had healed him—and Jesus had already left.

The leaders knew it must have been Jesus who had healed this man and who had told him to carry his bed on the Sabbath. Because Jesus didn't pay attention to their rules and traditions about how to keep the Sabbath holy, these religious leaders plotted all the more how they might stop Jesus' work. They were especially angry that on the Sabbath He helped people who were sick or in trouble.

One Sabbath, Jesus and His disciples were walking through a field of grain. The disciples were hungry, so they picked some of the heads of grain, rubbed them between their hands, and ate the kernels. Some strict Pharisees, who were spying on the disciples, saw this. They considered what the disciples had done to be breaking the Sabbath commandment. They said the disciples were threshing grain, and thus they were working on the Sabbath.

These Pharisees stopped Jesus and said, "Why are you doing what is not lawful to do on the Sabbath?"

Jesus answered, "Have you not even read this, what David did when he was hungry, he and those who were with him: how he went into the house of God, took and ate the showbread, and also gave some to those with him, which is not lawful for any but the priests to eat?" Then Jesus said, "The Son of Man is also Lord of the Sabbath."

Jesus wanted to teach the people that the Sabbath was to be a day of happiness—not a burden. But the Pharisees hated Jesus all the more because He spoke the truth.

On another Sabbath, Jesus was teaching in a synagogue, and there was a man in the congregation who had a withered hand. The Pharisees were whispering among themselves, wondering if Jesus would heal this man on the Sabbath. If so, they would accuse him of breaking the Sabbath commandment.

Jesus knew that His enemies were watching Him, and He knew also what they were thinking. He called to the man, "Arise and stand here." The man got up and stood before Jesus. The hand he shielded was pale and shrunken.

Then the Master said to the Jewish leaders, "I

THOUGHT QUESTION:
How does keeping the Sabbath help us in our walk with God?

will ask you one thing: Is it lawful on the Sabbath to do good or to do evil, to save life or to destroy?"

The Jewish leaders did not say a word. Then Jesus said to the man, "Stretch out your hand!" The man held out his hand, and when he did so, it was strong and firm like his other hand! Jesus had healed him. The leaders were furious and discussed among themselves what they could do to stop the Savior's work.

While His enemies were plotting against Him, Jesus went out of the city to a quiet spot on the side of a mountain and prayed all night. He asked His heavenly Father to give Him strength to help people and to save them from sin. He knew, too, that He must have power to meet His enemies who were becoming stronger and who would someday stop His work.

THE COURAGE OF JOHN THE BAPTIST

Matthew 11; Mark 6:16–29; Luke 7:16–35; 13:31, 32

Everyone in Judea was excited about the amazing work of Jesus of Nazareth. As the people saw Him healing the sick, raising the dead, and casting evil spirits out of individuals, some said that a great prophet had surely come among them. It wasn't long before the disciples of John the Baptist carried the news about what Jesus was doing to their master.

John was now in serious trouble. King Herod, son of the cruel ruler who had tried to kill Jesus when He was a baby, had married Herodias, the wife of another man. When John pointed out Herod's sin, the king was afraid, knowing that what John said was true. To ease his troubled conscience, Herod had John thrown into prison.

As John lay in prison, he began to wonder if Jesus really was the Messiah everyone had been looking for. If Jesus had come to save Israel, John thought, why didn't Jesus rescue him from prison? After all, John was Jesus' cousin.

Finally, after John had thought about the matter for some time, he sent two of his disciples to Jesus. When these men came to the Master, they found Him healing the sick and giving sight to the blind.

"John the Baptist has sent us to You, saying, 'Are You the Coming One, or do we look for another?' "

Jesus heard the question John's disciples asked, but He didn't answer them right away. He just kept on healing the sick people who crowded around Him while John's disciples watched. At last, Jesus took time to answer the two visitors. He said, "Go and tell John the things you have seen and heard: that the blind see, the lame walk, the lepers are cleansed, the deaf hear, the dead are raised, the poor have the gospel preached to them. And blessed is he who is not offended because of Me."

When John's disciples left, Jesus turned to the crowd and said, "I say to you, among those born of women, there is not a greater prophet than John the Baptist; but he who is least in the kingdom of God is greater than he."

John's disciples went back to visit their master in prison and to tell him the message from Jesus. When John heard what they had to say, he felt better and knew that the Messiah truly had come.

QUICK FACT:

Herodias sent her daughter to the banquet on purpose to trick Herod into killing John the Baptist.

Jesus never saw John the Baptist again. Soon afterwards, King Herod held a feast on his birthday for the officials of his court and other leading men of Galilee. During the banquet, Salome, the daughter of Herodias, danced before the guests. King Herod and his friends were so delighted that the king said to the girl, "Ask me whatever you want, and I will give it to you. . . . Whatever you ask me, I will give you, up to half of my kingdom."

Salome left and talked with her mother. Herodias had been waiting for such a moment. She hated John the Baptist because he had spoken the truth about her unlawful marriage to the king. So when her daughter said, "What shall I ask?" the mother replied, "The head of John the Baptist."

The girl hurried back to the king and said, "I want you to give me at once the head of John the Baptist on a platter."

The king was very, very sorry that he had made such a rash prom-

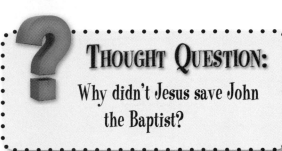

THOUGHT QUESTION:
Why didn't Jesus save John the Baptist?

ise to the girl, but he immediately sent one of his guards to the prison with orders to take the prophet's life. The soldier returned with the prophet's head on a platter and gave it to Salome, who carried it to her mother. John's disciples took the body of their beloved master and buried it.

Jesus knew how courageous John the Baptist had been to point out Herod's sin. When Jesus heard that the prophet was dead, He was sad. He said to His disciples, "Come aside by yourselves to a deserted place and rest a while."

Sometime later, certain Pharisees came to Jesus and said, "Get out and depart from here, for Herod wants to kill You." It was true, there were rumors that Herod was watching the work of the Mighty Prince, because he was afraid that Jesus was John come back from the dead. The wicked king said, "This is John, whom I beheaded; he has been raised from the dead!"

When the Pharisees told Him that Herod wanted to kill Him, Jesus replied, "Go, tell that fox, 'Behold, I cast out demons and perform cures today and tomorrow, and the third day I shall be perfected.'" By this Jesus meant that the king could never stop His work. The day would come when Jesus would stand before Herod, but not until the Messiah had completed His mission on earth.

Many of the Jewish leaders refused to obey John's call to repentance or to pay attention to Jesus' words of salvation.

Jesus had healed the sick and performed other wonderful works in the towns of Capernaum, Chorazin, and Bethsaida, but the people had not turned to God with all their hearts.

Jesus warned the people of these towns, saying,

> "Woe to you, Chorazin! Woe to you, Bethsaida! For if the mighty works which were done in you had been done in Tyre and Sidon, they would have repented long ago in sackcloth and ashes. But I say to you, it will be more tolerable for Tyre and Sidon in the day of judgment than for you. And you, Capernaum, who are exalted to heaven, will be brought down to Hades; for if the mighty works which were done in you had been done in Sodom, it would have remained until this day. But I say to you that it shall be more tolerable for the land of Sodom in the day of judgment than for you."

Then Jesus lifted His voice in prayer, saying, "I thank You, Father, Lord of heaven and earth, that You have hidden these things from the wise and prudent and have revealed them to babes. Even so, Father, for so it seemed good in Your sight."

The Master looked at the crowd of people who were listening to His words. With tenderness and love, He invited them to find peace and happiness in Him. He said, "Come to Me, all you who labor and are heavy laden, and I will give you rest. Take My yoke upon you and learn from Me, for I am gentle and lowly in heart, and you will find rest for your souls. For My yoke is easy and My burden is light."

He invites you and me today to do the same. If we accept Jesus' invitation and follow Him, we will find true happiness.

JESUS GOES TO A FEAST

Matthew 13:1–23; Luke 7:36–50; 15

Simon, a wealthy Pharisee, greatly admired Jesus and invited Him to a feast at his house. Simon lived in Bethany, a little town near Jerusalem. The Savior had once healed Simon of leprosy, so naturally Simon loved the Man who had saved his life.

While the guests were eating at the feast, a woman slipped into the room and knelt beside the Master as He sat at the table. Most of the people in the town knew this woman and thought she was a bad person. They refused to speak to her. But she had listened to Jesus talking about the importance of love. She had accepted Jesus into her heart, and He had gladly forgiven her sins.

As this woman knelt at Jesus' feet, she began to cry, and her tears fell on the Master's feet. Then she wiped His feet with her long, flowing hair. Afterward, she took perfume from a small box she was carrying and put it on His feet as a sign of how much she loved Him.

Now when Simon saw what was happening, he said to himself, "This man, if He were a prophet, would know who and what manner of woman this is who is touching Him, for she is a sinner."

Jesus turned to Simon and said, "Simon, I have something to say to you."

"Teacher, say it," the Pharisee replied. He thought he was a good person, and he was sure Jesus was going to say something nice about him.

"There was a certain creditor," Jesus began, "who had two debtors. One owed five hundred denarii, and the other fifty. And when they had nothing with which to repay, he freely forgave them both. Tell Me, therefore, which of them will love him more?"

Simon listened carefully and answered, "I suppose the one whom he forgave more."

"You have rightly judged," said Jesus.

Then turning to the woman, Jesus asked Simon, "Do you see this woman? I entered your house; you gave Me no water for My feet, but she has washed My feet with her tears and wiped them with the hair of her head. . . . You did not anoint My head with oil, but this woman has anointed My feet with fragrant oil. Therefore, I say to you, her sins, which are many, are forgiven, for she has loved much. But to whom little is forgiven, the same loves little."

GOD SAYS:

"Wherever this gospel is preached in the whole world, what this woman has done will also be told." –Mark 14:9

Then Jesus looked at the woman who was still kneeling at His feet. "Your sins are forgiven," He said to her.

Jesus told many parables or stories to help people understand God's wonderful love for men and women, boys and girls.

One time, when a group of Pharisees and scribes came to hear Him, Jesus said, "What man of you, having a hundred sheep, if he loses one of them, does not leave the ninety-nine in the wilderness, and go after the one which is lost until he finds it? And when he has found it, he lays it on his shoulders, rejoicing. And when he comes home, he calls together his friends and neighbors, saying to them, 'Rejoice with me, for I have found my sheep which was lost!' I say to you that likewise there will be more joy in heaven over one sinner who repents than over ninety-nine just persons who need no repentance."

The people listened to Jesus' stories carefully. They listened as he told them the thrilling story of a runaway boy. He said,

"A certain man had two sons. And the younger of them said to his father, 'Father, give me the portion of goods that falls to me.' So he divided to them his livelihood. And not many days after, the younger son gathered all together, journeyed to a far country, and there wasted his possessions with prodigal living.

"But when he had spent all, there arose a severe famine in that land, and he began to be in want. Then he went and joined himself to a citizen of that country, and he sent him into his fields to feed swine. And he would gladly have filled his stomach with the pods that the swine ate, and no one gave him anything.

"But when he came to himself, he said, 'How many of my father's hired servants have bread enough and to spare, and I perish with hunger! I will arise and go to my father, and will say to him, "Father, I have sinned against heaven and before you, and I am no longer worthy to be called your son. Make me like one of your hired servants."'

"And he arose and came to his father. But when he was still a great way off, his father saw him and had compassion, and ran and fell on his neck and kissed him. "And the son said to him, 'Father, I have sinned against heaven and in your sight, and am no longer worthy to be called your son.'

"But the father said to his servants, 'Bring out the best robe and put it on him, and put a ring on his hand and sandals on his feet. And bring the fatted calf here and kill it, and let us eat and be merry; for this my son was dead and is alive again; he was lost and is found.' "

THOUGHT QUESTION:

Why did Jesus use parables to teach the people about God?

Jesus told this story to show how much the Father in heaven loves us and how He is calling His children back to Him. If we confess our sins, our Savior is faithful to forgive us all our sins, and He will accept us back into the family of heaven.

One day when Jesus was by the Sea of Galilee, the people came crowding about Him. As the crowd grew larger, Jesus climbed into a fishing boat that was by the shore and sat down. Looking at the hillside, the Master saw a farmer planting grain in a field a little distance away. Jesus said,

"Behold, a sower went out to sow. And as he sowed, some seed fell by the wayside; and the birds came and devoured them. Some fell on stony places, where they did not have much earth; and they immediately sprang up because they had no depth of earth. But when the sun was up they were scorched, and because they had no root they withered away. And some fell among thorns, and the thorns sprang up and choked them. But others fell on good ground and yielded a crop: some a hundred-fold, some sixty, some thirty."

After the crowd had left and Jesus was alone, the disciples came to Him and wanted to know why He always taught with stories and parables. Jesus told them that it was not easy for the people to understand the kingdom of God, and stories helped make the truths clear and plain to them. Then He explained to the disciples the story of the sower and the seeds. Jesus said,

"When anyone hears the word of the kingdom, and does not understand it, then the wicked one comes and snatches away what was sown in his heart. This is he who received seed by the wayside. But he who received the seed on stony places, this is he who hears the word and immediately receives it with joy; yet he has no root in himself, but endures only for a while. For when tribulation or persecution arises because of the word, immediately he stumbles. Now he who received seed among the thorns is he who hears the word, and the cares of this world and the deceitfulness of riches

QUICK FACT:
The weeds and thorns are those things in our lives that crowd out Jesus.

choke the word, and he becomes unfruitful. But he who received seed on the good ground is he who hears the word and understands it, who indeed bears fruit and produces: some a hundredfold, some sixty, some thirty."

Many people heard the words of Jesus, but some quickly forgot them. Others loved riches more than they loved God, and they would not allow the seeds of truth to grow in their minds. Only a few of the people in the crowds that followed Jesus obeyed His teaching and followed Him.

The disciples were with the Master every day and were learning of the kingdom of heaven. The seeds of truth planted in their hearts would produce a rich harvest in years to come.

A STORMY SEA AND TWO MADMEN

Matthew 8:23–34; Mark 4:35–5:20

After Jesus had told stories to the crowd by the Sea of Galilee, He got into a fishing boat with His disciples to sail across the lake. The disciples pushed the little boat out into the water, and a stiff breeze sent it scudding over the waves.

The Master was tired after teaching the people all day and healing the sick and having crowds of people all around him listening to everything He said. He was so tired that He quickly fell asleep in the little boat as it crossed the lake.

After sunset, a fierce storm swept down from the mountains around the lake. Such storms often arose and blew the water into huge waves. Now the waves were so high they were sweeping into the boat and threatening to sink it.

Several of the disciples were strong fishermen who had spent years on the Sea of Galilee. But the storm was so bad, these strong disciples were afraid they couldn't keep the boat from sinking. They were being tossed around like a chip of wood, and it seemed that everyone on board the boat was going to die.

The disciples were working so hard to save the boat from sinking that they forgot all about Jesus. All at once they thought about Him. But where was He? In the darkness they cried, "Lord, save us! We are perishing!"

Jesus woke up. He turned to the disciples and said, "Why are you fearful, O you of little faith?" Then He stood up in the boat right in the middle of the terrible storm, and spoke to the angry winds and the sea. "Peace, be still!" He commanded. Immediately everything was quiet and calm. The wind stopped blowing, and the waves no longer smashed over the sides of the boat. There was a great calm over the sea.

The disciples looked at one another and began to breathe easier once more. They whispered to each other, "Who can this be, that even the winds and the sea obey Him?"

Morning brought a beautiful sunrise over the calm sea. It seemed to the disciples that the great storm in the night had been a dream, but they knew all too well that it had been real and that they would have drowned if Jesus had not been with them.

> ## GOD SAYS:
> "He calms the storm, so that its waves are still." –Psalm 107:29

The boat landed on the shore of a lonely, desolate region in the land of the Gadarenes. Jesus and His disciples went ashore and climbed the trail that led upward among the steep, rocky cliffs. A herd of pigs was feeding on the mountainside, and higher up on the rocky slopes was a graveyard.

As Jesus and His followers climbed the rough path, two madmen rushed upon them as if to tear them to pieces. The wild-looking men had cut themselves climbing over the sharp rocks, and their flesh was torn and bleeding. Pieces of chain were hanging from their arms and legs, for they had been chained up before they escaped to live among the tombs of this cemetery.

The disciples saw the madmen and turned to race back down the path toward the boat. But when they reached the shore, they found that Jesus was not with them. He was still standing on the path, talking to the men.

"What have we to do with You, Jesus, You Son of God?" screamed one of the madmen. "Have You come here to torment us before the time?"

"What is your name?" asked Jesus.

"My name is Legion," shrieked the demon-possessed man, "for we are many." It was true that many demons had taken control of these two men. The evil spirits begged Jesus not to cast them out. Finally these demons said, "Send us to the swine, that we may enter them."

THOUGHT QUESTION: Why were the disciples afraid during the storm when Jesus was with them?

"Go," Jesus ordered them. And the evil spirits came out of the two men and went into the pigs. Suddenly the whole herd of pigs rushed over the steep bank into the sea and drowned.

Some men had been taking care of the herd of pigs, and when they saw this, they ran to the nearby town and told everyone what had happened.

QUICK FACT: The two men whom Jesus cast the demons out of became the first missionaries in the region of Decapolis.

The people of the town hurried to meet Jesus. When they saw Him, they begged Him to leave their country. These people missed the opportunity of hearing Jesus because they thought more of their herd of pigs than they did of the two men who had been restored to their sound minds.

The men out of whom the evil spirits had been cast wanted to go with Jesus when He left, but He told them, "Go home to your friends, and tell them what great things the Lord has done for you, and how He has had compassion on you."

These men became the first missionaries for Jesus in their country, and as they went from town to town, telling everyone what the Master had done for them, the people were amazed and listened carefully.

JESUS AND A GIRL AND A BOY

Mark 5:21–43; 6:31–44

As the little fishing boat sailed back across the Sea of Galilee from the land of the Gadarenes, the disciples talked about the peace that Jesus gave. In stormy times, when the wind and the waves were angry, He could bring a deep calm. When men were crazed by evil spirits or when they were in sorrow, He could give peace of mind. What a wonderful Master they followed! Truly He was the Mighty Prince!

As the boat neared the little harbor from which they had sailed the evening before, Jesus and the disciples saw many people standing on the shore. They were waiting for the Man of Nazareth to return. Suddenly a man came running to the shore, and the crowd fell back to let him through. It was Jairus, an important man in the synagogue. When he saw Jesus, he fell at His feet and pleaded, "My little daughter lies at the point of death. Come and lay Your hands on her, that she may be healed, and she will live."

GOD SAYS:

" 'Daughter, your faith has made you well. Go in peace, and be healed of your affliction.' " –Mark 5:34

Jesus agreed to go with Jairus, and they started at once toward his home. Jesus' disciples followed them, as did many of the people who had been waiting for Jesus.

In the crowd was a woman who had been sick for twelve years. She had gone to many doctors and had spent all of her money trying to get well, but she had only grown worse. On this day she had been waiting to see Jesus, but Jairus's urgent request had caused the Master to hurry away. The woman felt that her chance for healing was gone, but she pushed forward to be as close to Jesus as possible. As He passed near her, she reached out and touched His robe. Immediately, she knew she had been cured of her sickness.

The Master stopped and turned around. "Who touched My clothes?" He asked.

The disciples looked at Him in amazement, and the people laughed. "You see the multitude thronging You, and You say, 'Who touched Me?' " they said.

Jesus continued looking for one person in that large crowd. The woman who had been sick came near and bowed before the Master, admitting that she had touched Him.

"Daughter," Jesus told her, "your faith has made you well. Go in peace, and be healed of your affliction."

Then as Jairus was trying to hurry Jesus along toward his house, one of his servants came running up. "Your daughter is dead," he told Jairus. "Why trouble the Teacher any farther?"

"Do not be afraid," said Jesus, "only believe."

Soon they arrived at the house and found hired mourners were already weeping, and flute players were making sad music because the twelve-year-old girl had died. When Jesus saw the confusion and the people weeping and wailing, He said, "Why make this commotion and weep? The child is not dead, but sleeping."

The people laughed at Him, but He told all the mourners and flute players and everyone else to leave. Then, Jesus and three of His disciples—Peter, James, and John—along with Jairus and his wife, went into the room where the girl lay.

Yes, she was dead. The girl was pale and still, beyond the help of any doctor. But Jesus took her by the hand and said to her, "Little girl, I say to you, arise."

Peter, James, and John looked at one another. Jesus, who had calmed the sea, was now speaking to a dead girl! Would she hear His voice and come back to life? The little girl's eyes fluttered open! She raised her head and then sat up! Her cheeks were rosy, and she smiled and held out her arms to her mother. It was as if she had been asleep and the Savior had awakened her.

QUICK FACT:
When Jesus comes again, everyone who died loving Him will be raised to life again at the sound of Jesus' voice.

The Bible promises that when Jesus comes again, everyone who has loved Him and has been laid to sleep in their graves will hear His voice speaking to them—just as Jairus's daughter did—and they will be raised to life again. They will live forever in the new home Jesus has prepared for them.

Jesus told the father and mother to give their daughter something to eat, and He also commanded them not to tell anyone what had happened. But this wonderful miracle could not be kept secret, and soon everyone in the region heard how the dead girl had been restored to life.

Another time, Jesus and His disciples sailed once again on the Sea of Galilee to a secluded spot where they could rest. But the crowds of people soon followed on foot along the lakeshore. When Jesus saw the crowds coming to Him, He felt sorry for them. They seemed like sheep looking for a shepherd. So, He taught the people about the kingdom of heaven, and He healed everyone who was sick.

When the sun was low, the disciples said to Jesus, "This is a deserted place, and already the hour is late. Send them away, that they may go into the surrounding country and villages and buy themselves bread; for they have nothing to eat."

"You give them something to eat," Jesus replied, not wanting to send the crowd away hungry.

"Shall we go and buy two hundred denarii worth of bread and give them something to eat?" the disciples wanted to know. They didn't have much money.

"How many loaves do you have?" Jesus asked. Then He added, "Go and see."

The disciples went around to the crowd of people to see if anyone had any food. They found a boy who had five little loaves of bread and two fish. But they knew that little lunch wouldn't begin to feed all these people.

Jesus told them to have the people sit down on the grassy hillside. When the people were sitting down, Jesus looked out over about five thousand people who had gathered to hear Him speak.

Then the Master took the five little loaves of bread and the two small fish, and He offered a prayer of thanks to His Father. He broke the loaves of bread into pieces, and He divided the fish into pieces and gave them to His disciples who went through the crowd distributing the food. They just kept handing out the food! There was no end to the bread and fish; there was plenty for everyone. When the disciples reached into the basket to give food to the hungry people, they always found there was more in the basket for the next hungry group.

THOUGHT QUESTION:
What important lesson did the disciples learn from the miracle of the loaves and fishes?

After everyone had eaten all they could hold, Jesus told His disciples to pick up all the food that was left so that nothing would be wasted. They gathered up twelve baskets full of bread and fish that were left over from the little boy's lunch of five loaves of bread and two fish!

A generous little boy helped Jesus feed five thousand people that day! Every boy and girl can help Jesus, and He will bless them if they serve Him with loving hearts.

A VISION OF GLORY

Matthew 14:22–36; 16:13–28; 17:1–9

When the multitude of restless people saw that Jesus could cure sick people, bring the dead back to life, and feed thousands of hungry men, women, and children with only a few loaves and two fish, they said, "This is truly the Prophet who is to come into the world!" Many of the people were certain that Jesus would drive the Roman soldiers out of the country and take the throne of Israel. They not only talked about making Him king, they even made plans to carry Him off to Jerusalem and set Him on the throne!

The twelve disciples dreamed of being high officers in the kingdom. Peter wondered what reward he would have for leaving his fishing boat to follow Jesus. Judas, who carried the money, thought only of wealth and honor, while James and John imagined that they would sit next to the Master on His throne—one on His right side and one on His left.

One evening, at the close of a busy day of helping the people who flocked around Him, Jesus wanted to be alone. Sending His disciples across the Sea of Galilee in a boat, Jesus dismissed the hundreds of people who pressed close to Him. Then, He climbed the path that led up the mountainside until He was by Himself, and He knelt in prayer.

During the night a strong wind arose on the lake, and the sea was rough and choppy. As the disciples were tossed about in their small boat, they longed for Jesus to help them. They remembered how He had calmed the angry winds and waves when another terrible storm had swept down on them and their little boat.

Jesus knew that His disciples needed Him, so toward morning He went to them, walking on the water of the lake! When the disciples saw Him, they were frightened and shouted one to another, "It is a ghost!"

Jesus heard their screams of fear and immediately called to them, "Be of good cheer! It is I; do not be afraid."

Peter leaned forward and shouted above the roar of the wind, "Lord, if it is You, command me to come to You on the water."

Back across the waves came Jesus' encouraging reply, "Come."

Peter jumped out of the boat and walked on the water toward Jesus. He was thrilled to think that he was doing what no other human being had ever done before! He looked around, hoping that the other disciples were watching him and envying him.

As soon as he took his eyes off Jesus, Peter felt the wind and heard its wild moan. He became frightened and began to sink into the white-capped waves. All the pride went out of him, and he cried out, "Lord, save me!"

Jesus was by his side in a moment. He caught hold of Peter's arm and lifted him up. "O you of little faith," Jesus said to him, "why did you doubt?"

Jesus and Peter got into the boat, and the wind stopped blowing, and the sea was calm. Then the disciples knelt

THOUGHT QUESTION:
Why did Peter begin to sink?

before their Master and said, "Truly You are the Son of God."

When Jesus and His disciples landed on the shores of the country of Gennesaret the next morning, people from all the surrounding towns and villages came to the Savior. They brought sick people to Him and begged Him to let the sick people just touch the edge of his robe, because everyone who touched even a piece of his clothes was cured.

About this time Jesus visited the northern cities of Caesarea Philippi. As He was walking along with His disciples, Jesus asked them, "Who do men say that I, the Son of Man, am?"

The disciples were quick to answer. "Some say John the Baptist, some Elijah, and others Jeremiah or one of the prophets."

For a few moments the little group walked along in silence, wondering what Jesus was thinking. Then the Master turned and looked straight at the men who knew Him best. "But who do you say that I am?" He asked them.

Simon Peter was always ready to speak first. He answered boldly, "You are the Christ, the Son of the living God!"

A smile touched the Master's face, and He said, "Blessed are you, Simon Bar-Jonah, for flesh and blood has not revealed this to you, but My Father who is in heaven." How happy it made the Master to know that His disciples had faith in Him! It still takes faith today to follow Jesus.

Jesus knew that before long He would go to Jerusalem, where He would be put on trial and be punished and, lastly, be put to death. He knew, too, that the disciples would be confused and shocked when that happened. So the Master decided to explain to them what was coming in order to prepare them for the crisis.

THOUGHT QUESTION:

Why was it important for the people to know that Jesus was the Son of God and not just a prophet?

He told them how He would suffer at the hands of the high priest and be killed. He told them how He would be raised to life again on the third day.

The disciples looked at one another, perplexed and worried. Peter took Jesus by the arm and led Him aside and reproved Him, saying, "Far be it from You, Lord; this shall not happen to You!"

Jesus turned to Peter and said sharply, "Get behind Me, Satan! You are an offense to Me, for you are not mindful of the things of God, but the things of men."

Again and again, the Master was tempted by Satan to take the easy way out—to save Himself from dying on the cross. Jesus needed all the courage and strength He could find to help Him face death, but now Peter was talking doubt and discouragement. Satan was using Peter to try to tempt Jesus to bypass the cross.

Six days later, Jesus invited Peter, James, and John to go with Him to the top of a high mountain. There a wonderful change in Jesus' appearance took place. His face shone bright like the sun, and His clothes became as white as light. Two great men of Old Testament times —Moses and Elijah— appeared beside Jesus, and they talked with the Lord.

QUICK FACT:
In Jewish times worship involved building a special place to offer prayers and sacrifices.

Peter, James, and John saw this wonderful sight, but they didn't understand what they were seeing. They were bewildered and in awe. Peter spoke up without thinking about what he was saying. "Lord," he said to Jesus, "it is good for us to be here; if You wish, let us make here three tabernacles: one for You, one for Moses, and one for Elijah."

But Peter's words were cut off as a bright cloud overshadowed them and a Voice from the cloud said, "This is My beloved Son, in whom I am well pleased. Hear Him!"

The three disciples fell to the ground, trembling with fear. Jesus came and helped them up, saying, "Arise, and do not be afraid." When the disciples looked up, they saw no one standing there except Jesus.

In stunned silence the three men followed their Master down the mountain. Jesus cautioned them, saying, "Tell the vision to no one until the Son of Man is risen from the dead."

Years later, the disciples remembered what they had seen. In one of his letters to the church, a much older Peter wrote of how he had seen the majesty and glory of Jesus on the mountaintop and how he had heard the Voice from heaven say, "This is My beloved Son, in whom I am well pleased."

This wonderful vision helped the disciples realize that Jesus was indeed the Messiah that the prophets had predicted would come. They realized, too, that Jesus was the Mighty Prince from a glorious kingdom far beyond this earth.

Loving God and Helping Our Neighbors

Matthew 17:24–27; 19:16–23; Luke 10:25–37; John 7:10–51; 9:1–10:39

It was autumn. The grain had been harvested. The fruit had been gathered. And now it was time for the people to offer their thanks to God for all the blessings He had given them. The Feast of Tabernacles—a happy festival of thanksgiving— was about to take place at Jerusalem.

Thousands of people journeyed to the capital city for the celebration. The feast lasted eight days, and during this time the people lived in little booths set up in the streets and on the flat roofs of houses. They did this to remember how their ancestors had lived in tents in the wilderness for forty years after they fled from Egypt, and how God had brought them safely into the land of Canaan.

Jesus decided that He would attend the Feast of Tabernacles in Jerusalem, although He knew that His enemies there were plotting to kill Him. In fact, the rulers in Jerusalem had sent out men to follow Jesus around and try to catch Him breaking the religious laws.

One day, while the disciples were in Capernaum, some tax collectors came to Peter and asked, "Does your Teacher not pay the temple tax?"

Without thinking, Peter answered, "Yes."

But when Peter went home, Jesus, who knew about Peter's conversation with the tax collectors, said to him, "What do you think, Simon? From whom do the kings of the earth take customs or taxes, from their own sons or from strangers?"

"From strangers," Peter replied.

"Then the sons are free," Jesus said thoughtfully. He wanted to impress Peter with the fact that although He and the disciples were loyal to the temple, they should also remember that priests and prophets were exempt from this temple tax. So if Jesus paid the tax, it would be admitting that He wasn't really a prophet or teacher.

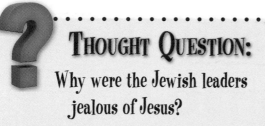

THOUGHT QUESTION:

Why were the Jewish leaders jealous of Jesus?

Peter realized his mistake, and he regretted his hasty answer—that, of course, Jesus would pay the tax. Jesus rescued Peter from the difficult situation, however. He told him, "Nevertheless, lest we offend them, go to the sea, cast in a hook, and take the fish that comes up first. And when you have opened its mouth, you will find a piece of money; take that and give it to them for Me and you."

Peter did just what Jesus told him to do. And, sure enough, there was a coin in the mouth of the first fish he caught! Soon the money was in the tax collector's hands. Once more, the Pharisees who tried to trap Jesus had met defeat.

When Jesus arrived at Jerusalem for the Feast of Tabernacles, there was already a crowd in town. Groups of people stood in the streets talking about Him. Some said that Jesus was a good man, and others argued that He was a deceiver.

One morning during the feast, Jesus walked calmly into the temple and began to teach. Many of the Jewish leaders were astonished at the courage of this Man of Nazareth, for they knew that His enemies were plotting to kill Him. Some of the people said, "Is this not He whom they seek to kill? But look! He speaks boldly, and they say nothing to Him. Do the rulers know indeed that this is truly the Christ?"

On the last day of the feast Jesus stood before the crowd in the court of the temple and said, "If anyone thirsts, let him come to Me and drink. He who believes in Me, as the Scripture has said, out of his heart will flow rivers of living water." Jesus meant that when a person is willing, God's Spirit comes into his heart and helps him to be kind and loving.

When the people heard these words, some of them said, "Truly, this is the Prophet."

Others said, "This is the Christ."

The people weren't sure whether Jesus was the Messiah, but they all knew He was a very special person. The priests and rulers decided it was time to put Him in jail, but Nicodemus, a Pharisee who had visited with Jesus secretly and had learned the truth about God's kingdom, said to his fellow rulers, "Does our law judge a man before it hears him and knows what he is doing?"

QUICK FACT: The Jews believed that if something bad happened to you, such as becoming blind or getting leprosy, it was because you had sinned.

The next Sabbath, after Jesus had been to the temple, He and His disciples were walking through the streets of Jerusalem when they saw a man who had been blind from his birth. When the disciples saw this poor beggar making his way as best he could, they said, "Rabbi, who sinned, this man or his parents, that he was born blind?"

Jesus answered, "Neither this man nor his parents sinned, but that the works of God should be revealed in him." As he spoke, the Master spit on the dusty ground and made clay with the saliva. Then He went to the blind man and put the clay on his eyes. "Go, wash in the pool of Siloam," Jesus told him.

Down the rough street the blind man went, eagerly groping his way toward the pool. After a time he returned to his house, and the neighbors and people who had seen him begging were amazed.

"Is not this he who sat and begged?" they asked one another.

Some thought it was the blind man. Others said he looked like the blind man, but they weren't sure.

"I am he," shouted the man who had been blind.

"How were your eyes opened?" they wanted to know.

The beggar told his story, and then the people took him to the Pharisees. When these Jewish leaders heard the news, they knew it must have been Jesus who had healed the blind man. They were not pleased that Jesus had healed this man on the Sabbath, and they said about Jesus, "This Man is not from God, because He does not keep the Sabbath."

They argued and argued about whether the man had really been blind. Maybe there hadn't been a miracle at all. Finally they called the beggar's parents and asked them, "Is this your son, who you say was born blind? How then does he now see?"

"We know that this is our son, and that he was born blind," the parents replied, "but by what means he now sees we do not know, or who opened his eyes we do not know. He is of age; ask him. He will speak for himself."

The Pharisees were even more displeased and worried. They didn't want to admit that Jesus

> **GOD SAYS:**
> " 'My sheep hear My voice, and I know them, and they follow Me.' "
> –John 10:27

had healed a blind man, and they were not happy that the miracle had happened on the Sabbath. So they talked to the man who had been blind and told him he couldn't come to the synagogue any more. They threw him out of the church!

Later Jesus heard what they had done to this man. He went looking for him and found him. He spoke words of courage and faith to the man. The man accepted Jesus as the Messiah and worshiped Him.

When the rulers argued with Jesus about what He had done in healing the blind man, He said,

"I am the door of the sheep. All who ever came before Me are thieves and robbers, but the sheep did not hear them. I am the door. If anyone enters by Me, he will be saved, and will go in and out and find pasture. The thief does not come except to steal, and to kill, and to destroy. I have come that they may have life, and that they may have it more abundantly.

"I am the good shepherd. The good shepherd gives His life for the sheep. But a hireling, he who is not the shepherd, one who does not own the sheep, sees the wolf coming and leaves the sheep and flees; and the wolf catches the sheep and scatters them. The hireling flees because he is a hireling and does not care about the sheep. I am the good shepherd; and I know My sheep, and am known by My own. As the Father knows Me, even so I know the Father; and I lay down My life for the sheep. And other sheep I have which are not of this fold; them also I must bring, and they will hear My voice; and there will be one flock and one shepherd.

"Therefore My Father loves Me, because I lay down My life that I may take it again. No one takes it from Me, but I lay it down of Myself. I have power to lay it down, and I have power to take it again. This command I have received from My Father."

Finally the Jews said, "He has a demon and is mad." Then they picked up stones and would have killed Him, but Jesus disappeared and left the temple.

One day a lawyer who was expert in legal matters came to question Jesus. "Teacher," he said, "what shall I do to inherit eternal life?"

Jesus looked at the man and asked him a question in return, "What is written in the law? What is your reading of it?"

THOUGHT QUESTION:
Who does God consider "our neighbor?"

The lawyer replied, " 'You shall love the Lord your God with all your heart, with all your soul, with all your strength, and with all your mind,' and 'your neighbor as yourself.' "

"You have answered rightly," Jesus said, looking straight at the lawyer. "Do this and you will live."

But the lawyer was not satisfied with this answer, and he continued to question Jesus. "Who is my neighbor?" he asked.

For a moment Jesus said nothing, and then He began to tell the story of a man who had recently traveled from Jerusalem to Jericho. He "fell among thieves," Jesus said,

> "who stripped him of his clothing, wounded him, and departed, leaving him half dead. Now by chance a certain priest came down that road. And when he saw him, he passed by on the other side. Likewise a Levite, when he arrived at the place, came and looked, and passed by on the other side. But a certain Samaritan, as he journeyed, came where he was. And when he saw him, he had compassion on him. So he went to him and bandaged his wounds, pouring on oil and wine; and he set him on his own animal, brought him to an inn, and took care of him. On the next day, when he departed, he took out two denarii, gave them to the innkeeper,

and said to him, 'Take care of him; and whatever more you spend, when I come again, I will repay you.' "

As Jesus told the story, the lawyer was listening carefully. Now, Jesus turned and asked him, "Which of these three do you think was neighbor to him who fell among the thieves?"

"He who showed mercy on him," the lawyer replied quickly.

"Go and do likewise," Jesus said to him.

Jesus told this story to tell us that anyone who is in need is our neighbor. It makes no difference what his race or religion is—if a person needs help, we, as followers of Jesus Christ, are to do all we can for him.

The Savior loved both rich and poor people equally. He wanted the people who had plenty of money to love their neighbors enough to help them when they were in need. One day, while Jesus was walking down the road, a young man dressed in a beautiful robe came running up to Him and bowed politely. "Good Teacher," he said, "what good thing shall I do that I may have eternal life?"

"Why do you call Me good?" Jesus asked. "No one is good but One, that is, God. But if you want to enter into life, keep the commandments."

This young man knew the law from beginning to end, so he asked, "Which ones?"

Jesus said, " 'You shall not murder,' 'You shall not commit adultery,' 'You shall not steal,' 'You shall not bear false witness,' 'Honor your father and your mother,' and 'You shall love your neighbor as yourself.' "

"All these things I have kept from my youth," replied the rich young man. "What do I still lack?"

Jesus put the final test to the man. "If you want to be perfect," said Jesus, "go, sell what you have and give to the poor, and you will have treasure in heaven; and come, follow Me."

The man shook his head and went away disappointed and sad, because he had a lot of money and possessions. He was selfish and did not want to give his wealth to help the poor, nor did he want to follow Jesus.

As the Master watched the young man walk away, He said to His disciples, "Assuredly, I say to you that it is hard for a rich man to enter the kingdom of heaven."

When a person has lots of money, he can buy almost anything he wants. He trusts in himself and refuses to love God. That is why it is so difficult for a rich person to sacrifice himself and follow Jesus.

LEARNING TO LOVE

Matthew 18; 19:13–15; Luke 9:57–62; 10:1–24, 38–42

These were busy days for Jesus and His disciples. The Master knew that He had only a short time to finish His work, and there was so much to do. He needed more disciples who were loyal and true so that He could train them to give His message. It was not easy to follow Jesus, for one had to give up many things. One had to leave home and loved ones to give the good news of God's love to others.

One day a man met the Master on the road and said to Him, "I will follow You wherever You go."

"Foxes have holes and the birds of the air have nests, but the Son of Man has nowhere to lay His head," Jesus answered. He was testing the man to see if he would truly endure hardship as a faithful disciple.

Another day, a man came to the Savior and said, "Lord, I will follow You, but let me first go and bid them farewell who are at my house."

Jesus turned to the man and said bluntly, "No one, having put his hand to the plow, and looking back, is fit for the kingdom of God." Being Christ's disciple requires complete dedication.

When Jesus had gathered seventy disciples whom He could trust, He sent them out two by two to tell the good news of God's love. Before they started, He said to them, "The harvest truly is great, but the laborers are few; therefore pray the Lord of the harvest to send out laborers into His harvest. Go your way; behold, I send you out as lambs among wolves."

When the seventy disciples returned they had good results to report. They said excitedly, "Lord, even the demons are subject to us in Your name."

The Master was happy that His disciples had been faithful and true to Him. He saw that the powers of evil were being defeated. At that moment Jesus prayed, "I thank You, Father, Lord of heaven and earth."

GOD SAYS:

" 'If anyone desires to come after Me, let him deny himself, and take up his cross, and follow Me.' "

– Matthew 16:24

Then, turning to the seventy disciples, He said, "Blessed are the eyes which see the things you see; for I tell you that many prophets and kings have desired to see what you see, and have not seen it, and to hear what you hear, and have not heard it."

Jesus loved His friends and enjoyed being with them. At the village of Bethany, near Jerusalem, there was a home where He often stayed when He wanted a few quiet hours away from the crowds of people. Lazarus and his two sisters, Martha and Mary, lived there. Martha, the older sister, was a good housekeeper and was always cleaning, cooking, and worrying about housework. Her younger sister, Mary, enjoyed sitting and thinking; when Jesus came, she spent most of her time visiting with Him.

"Lord," said Martha, "do You not care that my sister has left me to serve alone? Therefore tell her to help me."

"Martha, Martha, you are worried and troubled about many things," Jesus answered quietly, looking straight into Martha's eyes. "But one things is needed, and Mary has chosen that good part, which will not be taken away from her."

Jesus did not mean that it was wrong to have a nice home or to keep it clean and tidy. He wanted to teach Martha that she shouldn't spend all her time thinking about housework, cooking, making clothes, and serving meals. There are more important things to be concerned about. We must take time to read the Bible and to pray. We must not think so much of ourselves that we don't have time to do kind acts for others and to show our friends that we love them. Our lives should follow the pattern Jesus has given us.

The people continued to whisper about Jesus being the king of Israel, and the disciples dreamed of being princes and rulers. One day they could not keep their secret thoughts to themselves any longer, so they asked Jesus, "Who then is greatest in the kingdom of heaven?"

The Master didn't answer right away. He called a little child to Him and asked him to stand in front of them. "I say to you," He told the disciples, "unless you are converted and become as little children, you will by no means enter the kingdom of heaven." Jesus wanted His disciples to be honest and true and to have simple faith—like a little child.

"Take heed that you do not despise one of these little ones," he continued, pointing to the child standing there, "for I say to you that in heaven their angels always see the face of my Father who is in heaven." Jesus was referring to the guardian angel who goes with each boy and girl, and each man and woman. Our guardian angel protects us and helps us to do right. Our angel can return to heaven and tell the Father about our needs.

Jesus loves boys and girls. While He was teaching, mothers would

QUICK FACT:
Jesus loved children and they loved Him—His kind eyes and gentle way made them want to be near Him.

bring their children to Him, and He would bless them. One day, several mothers came to Him with their children. The boys and girls surrounded Jesus, and some of the younger children had climbed on His lap. When the disciples saw this, they tried to shoo the youngsters away.

Jesus said, "Let the little children come to Me, and do not forbid them; for of such is the kingdom of heaven."

In God's kingdom those who are truly great are not rich or proud; the truly great are those who are kind and loving and unselfish—those who forgive the wrongs others do to them.

Peter wanted to know how to be kind and forgiving to those who wronged him. Jesus said, "If your brother sins against you, go and tell him his fault between you and him alone." This is a much better way to settle a misunderstanding than to go to everyone else and tell them how someone has mistreated you. "If he hears you," added Jesus, "you have gained your brother."

Peter wondered how this would work, and he asked, "Lord, how often shall my brother sin against me, and I forgive him? Up to seven times?" There was a common saying that a person should forgive someone three times. Peter thought he was being generous.

However, Jesus was quick to show that His followers must *always* be ready and willing to forgive. "I do not say to you, up to seven times, but up to seventy times seven," he told Peter. God loves us, and His forgiveness is endless. In the same way, we should forgive those who wrong us as often as necessary.

Then Jesus told a story of a king who decided to settle all his accounts with his servants. "When he had begun to settle accounts," Jesus began,

"one was brought to him who owed him ten thousand talents. But as he was not able to pay, his master commanded that he be sold, with his wife and children and all that he had, and that payment be made. The servant therefore fell down before him, saying, 'Master, have patience with me, and I will pay you all.' Then the master of that servant was moved with compassion, released him, and forgave him the debt.

"But that servant went out and found one of his fellow servants who owed him a hundred denarii; and he laid hands on him and took him by the throat, saying, 'Pay me what you owe!' So his fellow servant fell down at his feet and begged him, saying, 'Have patience with me, and I will pay you all.' And he would not, but went and threw him into prison till he should pay the debt. So when his fellow servants saw what had been done, they were very grieved, and came and told their master all that had been done. Then his master, after he had called him, said to him, 'You wicked servant! I forgave you all that debt because you begged me. Should not you also have had compassion on your fellow servant, just as I had pity on you?' "

THOUGHT QUESTION:
Why does God want us to always be willing to forgive?

Jesus told this story to show how willing God the Father is to forgive us all our sins—no matter how many or how great they are. But He also told the story to show us how important it is that we forgive those who have wronged us.

AT THE GRAVE OF LAZARUS

Luke 18:31–33; John 11

Jesus was teaching and healing the sick in Perea, an area east of the Jordan River where John had preached and baptized. One day, as the Savior was talking to the people and healing the sick, a messenger came hurrying up. "Lord," he said, "behold, he whom You love is sick." Mary and Martha, Jesus' friends who lived in Bethany, had sent this messenger to tell Jesus that their brother, Lazarus, was desperately ill.

Jesus loved Lazarus and his sisters, but when He received the news that His friend was sick, He stayed two more days in that area, preaching and teaching. The third day, He said to His disciples, "Let us go to Judea again."

The disciples were worried, for they knew His enemies in Judea were planning to kill Jesus. They said, "Rabbi, lately the Jews sought to stone You, and You are going there again?"

The Savior was not afraid of what His enemies might do. He wanted to go to the home of His friends and comfort them in their time of need. "Our friend Lazarus sleeps," Jesus told His disciples, "but I go that I may wake him up."

"Lord, if he sleeps he will get well," the disciples replied, for they thought Jesus meant Lazarus was resting and returning to health.

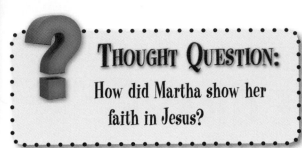

THOUGHT QUESTION:

How did Martha show her faith in Jesus?

"Lazarus is dead," said Jesus plainly. "And I am glad for your sakes that I was not there, that you may believe. Nevertheless, let us go to him."

Thomas, one of Jesus' disciples, shook his head sadly. He was sure that they were all going to die if they went to Jerusalem. He whispered to the other disciples, "Let us also go, that we may die with Him."

When Jesus arrived at Bethany, He found that Lazarus had been dead and buried for four days. Friends of Martha and Mary had come out from Jerusalem for the funeral, and some were still there, trying to comfort the sorrowing sisters. When Jesus and His disciples approached the village, Martha heard that the Master was coming, and she ran to meet Him. With tears in her eyes, she said, "Lord, if You had been here, my brother would not have died! But even now I know that whatever You ask of God, God will give You."

"Your brother will rise again," said Jesus reassuringly.

"I know that he will rise again in the resurrection at the last day," replied Martha.

Then Jesus tried to comfort her. "I am the resurrection and the life," He declared. "He who believes in Me, though he may die, he shall live." Then Jesus turned directly to Martha and asked, "Do you believe this?"

Through her tears Martha replied, "Yes, Lord, I believe that You are the Christ, the Son of God, who is to come into the world."

Then Martha hurried to her sister and whispered softly to her, "The Teacher has come and is calling for you."

When Mary came to where Jesus was, she fell at His feet and said the same thing Martha had said, "Lord, if You had been here, my brother would not have died!"

The sorrow and tears of the women were more than Jesus could bear, and He turned to Martha and Mary and asked quickly, "Where have you laid him?"

"Come and see," said the sisters. With tears in His eyes Jesus went with them to the tomb. He was crying, and the Jews who saw Him said, "See how He loved him!"

Arriving at the rocky hillside, the Master saw the cave where Lazarus was buried. A huge stone had been rolled against the opening to close the tomb. Jesus commanded, "Take away the stone." Martha reminded Jesus that Lazarus had been dead for four days.

"Did I not say to you that if you would believe you would see the glory of God?" Jesus asked.

The men pushed hard, and the stone was rolled away. Then Jesus prayed, "Father, I thank You that You have heard Me. And I know that You always hear Me, but because of the people who are standing by I said this, that they may believe that You sent Me." Then He called out loudly, "Lazarus, come forth!"

There was a moment of silence, and each person in the crowd held his breath. There was a stir within the darkness of the tomb, and then Lazarus came out, bound hand and foot with the white

Quick Fact:
Lazarus and his sisters were good friends of Jesus, and Jesus performed one of His greatest miracles for Lazarus.

burial sheet wound around him and a piece of cloth covering his face. The people were speechless, amazed, and happy. Mary and Martha stopped crying and threw their arms around their brother.

"Loose him, and let him go," Jesus commanded. Then Lazarus looked into the eyes of his Savior, and there was a huge smile on his lips.

But Jesus' enemies, who had seen Him raise Lazarus from the dead, soon lost sight of the wonder of this amazing miracle. They told the religious leaders in Jerusalem how Jesus had brought to life a man who had been dead for four days. And they knew that if such miracles continued, they would lose their influence with the people and that Jesus would be accepted as the Messiah. So, they began to plot even more furiously, how to kill the Son of God! They remembered how the Mighty Prince had driven the money changers from the temple. Some even remembered how the Boy Jesus had stood before them when He was twelve years old, asking them questions.

As they met together in council, one of the leaders said, "What shall we do? For this Man works many signs. If we let Him alone like this, everyone will believe in Him, and the Romans will come and take away both our place and nation."

Caiaphas, the high priest, said, "You know nothing at all, nor do you consider that it is expedient for us that one man should die for the people, and not that the whole nation should perish."

About this time, Jesus took His twelve disciples aside and talked with them quietly. He said, "Behold, we are going up to Jerusalem, and all things that are written by the prophets concerning the Son of Man will be accomplished. For He will be delivered to the Gentiles and will be mocked and insulted and spit upon. They will scourge Him and kill Him. And the third day He will rise again."

The disciples looked bewildered. They heard what He said, but they couldn't understand it. James and John were still thinking about high positions next to their King. And Judas gripped the money bag tighter, for he thought that when Jesus drove His enemies from the country there would be great riches for all the disciples. Little did these twelve men know what lay ahead. Little did they dream of the sorrow and fear that would fill their hearts in the days to come, for everything the Mighty Prince had predicted would happen just as He said it would.

ZACCHAEUS UP A TREE

Mark 10:32–52; Luke 19:1–44

After bringing Lazarus back to life, Jesus did not appear in public again among the Jews for some time, because they hated Him bitterly. For three years, He had healed the sick and had spoken to the crowds who came to Him. Now He took His disciples to a little town called Ephraim, on the edge of the desert, where He taught them many lessons concerning His kingdom.

It was springtime, and the first flowers were in bloom. The birds were singing, the grass was turning green, and the water in the brooks was tumbling down the canyons into the Jordan River. The Passover Feast was approaching, a time when thousands of people from every part of Israel traveled to Jerusalem. Jesus announced to His disciples that they would go to the temple for the Passover festival.

As they started toward Jerusalem, Jesus walked ahead; the disciples trailed behind, because they

109

were afraid. They knew they would face enemies in Jerusalem—enemies who were plotting the death of their Master.

The road they were following passed through the town of Jericho. As Jesus and His disciples came near the city, they saw a blind beggar named Bartimaeus, sitting near the gate. Bartimaeus had heard how Jesus healed sick people and opened the eyes of those who couldn't see; he longed to meet this Great Physician. He couldn't see Jesus coming, but he could hear the chatter of the crowd by the roadside, and he heard the people saying that Jesus was getting nearer.

Hope sprang up in this blind man's heart, and he began to shout, "Jesus, Son of David, have mercy on me!"

The people tried to make him be quiet, but the more they told him to hush, the louder he shouted.

Jesus stopped and told His disciples to bring the blind man to Him. Some of the man's friends said to him, "Be of good cheer. Rise, He is calling you." Bartimaeus jumped up quickly and groped his way toward Jesus with outstretched hands.

"What do you want Me to do for you?" asked the Master, testing him.

"Rabboni," answered Bartimaeus, "that I may receive my sight."

"Go your way," said Jesus. "Your faith has made you well."

THOUGHT QUESTION:

What obstacles do we have to overcome to see Jesus?

Immediately, Bartimaeus could see! And the very first thing he saw was the face of Jesus, the One who had healed him. Joyfully, he followed the Master down the road for a while.

In Jericho lived a rich man named Zacchaeus. The Jews disliked him because he collected taxes for the Romans. But even though he was a tax collector, Zacchaeus tried to be honest and kind. Most of all he longed to see Jesus. But he was short and couldn't see over the heads of the people. He knew it would be impossible to get a good view of the Mighty Prince in the narrow, crowded streets of Jericho, so he ran ahead and climbed into a sycamore tree.

QUICK FACT: By following the Jewish custom for a royal entry, Jesus declared Himself Israel's king.

When the Master came under the tree, He looked up into the branches and saw the man. "Zacchaeus, make haste and come down," He called, "for today I must stay at your house."

Zacchaeus was so surprised that he almost fell out of the tree! He quickly climbed down from the tree and welcomed the Savior. Some of the people raised their eyebrows and whispered about Jesus, "He has gone to be a guest with a man who is a sinner."

But Zacchaeus didn't care. He was so happy that he wanted to shout! He wanted to help everyone in the world. Suddenly, he turned to Jesus and said, "Look, Lord, I give half of my goods to the poor; and if I have taken anything from anyone by false accusation, I restore fourfold."

Jesus smiled and looked down at the little man. "Today salvation has come to this house," He declared. He was happy to find a rich man who was willing to share his money with the poor and the needy. The happiest man in Jericho that day was Zacchaeus, for Jesus Christ had come to his house as a guest.

Afterward, Jesus and His disciples continued their journey to Jerusalem. They passed through the village of Bethphage and came to the Mount of Olives. Everywhere, crowds of people who had arrived for the Passover were talking about Jesus. They were wondering if He would attend the feast. Soon the news spread through the streets of the city that the Man of Nazareth was coming, and hundreds of people flocked out through the gates of the city to find the Teacher.

As Jesus and His disciples rested on the Mount of Olives, He gave special instructions to two of His disciples. "Go into the village opposite you, where as you enter you will find a colt tied, on which no one has ever sat. Loose it and bring it here. And if anyone asks you, 'Why are you loosing it?' thus you shall say to him, 'Because the Lord has need of it.' "

The two disciples went to do as Jesus said, and when they found the colt tied in the street at the door of a house, they untied it. Some of the bystanders said to them, "Why are you loosing the colt?" The disciples answered as Jesus had told them to do, and the bystanders let them take the animal.

They brought the colt to Jesus and threw their coats over it. They helped Jesus sit on the colt, and He rode off toward Jerusalem. It was an old custom for kings to make a royal entrance into their capital city in this way.

By this time, the crowds had become so great that people were standing almost shoulder to shoulder all along the road as Jesus and His disciples moved toward the city. Some of the men and women spread their coats in front of Him on the road, while others cut leafy branches from nearby olive and palm trees and scattered the road before Him.

The children ran ahead, waving palm branches, and the crowds shouted,

        " 'Blessed is the King who comes in the name of the Lord!'

Peace in heaven and glory in the highest!' " (Luke 19:38).

When the religious leaders saw the shouting, singing crowd, they scowled and clenched their fists. Was this Man actually planning to be king? If so, what would happen to their influence over the people? If Jesus became king, how would they be able to keep on collecting money unfairly from the people?

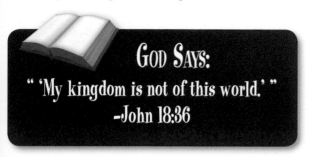

GOD SAYS:
" 'My kingdom is not of this world.' "
-John 18:36

As the joyful procession neared the city gates, Jesus looked at Jerusalem, and tears came to His eyes. He raised His hand and, waving it toward the city, said, "If you had known, even you, especially in this your day, the things that make for your peace! But now they are hidden from your eyes. For days will come upon you when your enemies will build an embankment around you, surround you and close you in on every side, and level you, and your children within you, to the ground; and they will not leave you one stone upon another because you did not know the time of your visitation."

Jesus was thinking of the time to come when the Roman army would march against the city and destroy it. Jerusalem would fall because its people had rejected God's offer of salvation and eternal life.

When Jesus entered the city, the people of Jerusalem were excited; everyone was wondering what would happen next. Was Jesus truly the Messiah who had been promised for so long? Would He declare Himself to be the King of Israel and deliver the nation from the Romans who occupied their country?

That evening, after His triumphal entry into Jerusalem, Jesus left the city and returned to Bethany to spend the night.

JESUS MEETS ENEMIES AND FRIENDS

Matthew 21:12–32; Mark 11:15–33; Luke 20; 21:1–4; John 12:20–50

The next morning, Jesus returned to Jerusalem and entered the temple. He saw the cattle stalls and the pigeon cages belonging to the traders who were doing a thriving business in the court of God's house. He heard the bleating of sheep, the mooing of cattle, and the clinking sound of coins.

Three years before, the Mighty Prince had driven these traders from the temple, and now, once again, He drove out those who were buying and selling. He upset the money-changers' tables, spilling their coins all over the floor. He turned over the chairs of those who were selling doves for offerings.

As Jesus stood in the temple court, His piercing eyes searched out His enemies, and no one dared question His authority. Except for a few of His disciples, Jesus stood alone. Then, turning to the crowd of people who had drawn back in fear and amazement, Jesus said, "Is it not written, 'My house shall be called a house of prayer for all nations'? But you have made it a 'den of thieves.' "

Then the sick and the blind and the crippled people pushed through the crowd of money changers and animal traders to find Jesus. They knew He would help them. Some children became so excited, they began calling out, "Hosanna to the Son of David!"

When the Pharisees and priests saw what had happened, they were very angry. They came to Jesus and pointed to the children who were praising Him, and said, "Do you hear what these are saying?" They wanted the children to be quiet and stop praising Jesus.

"Yes," Jesus answered. "Have you never read,

'Out of the mouth of babes and nursing infants
You have perfected praise'?" (Matthew 21:16).

During the Passover week Jesus taught the crowds of people who filled the temple courtyard. The priests and scribes wanted to arrest the Master, but they were afraid to do so because they knew the people loved Him. One day the leaders came to Jesus and began to question Him. "By what authority are You doing these things? And who gave You this authority?"

"I also will ask you one thing," Jesus replied, "which if you tell Me, I likewise will tell you by what authority I do these things: The baptism of John—where was it from. From heaven or from men?"

The group of priests and rulers whispered together for a moment. "If we say 'From heaven,' He will say to us, 'Why then did you not believe him?' But if we say, 'From men,' we fear the multitude, for all count John as a prophet."

Finally they turned back toward Jesus and said that they didn't know whether or not John's ministry was from heaven. Then Jesus looked straight at them and said, "Neither will I tell you by what authority I do these things."

Not long after this, some spies came to Jesus, pretending to be sincerely wanting His advice. They said, "Teacher, we know that You say and teach rightly, and You do not show personal fa-

GOD SAYS:
"Walk prudently when you go to the house of God." -Ecclesiastes 5:1

voritism, but teach the way of God in truth: Is it lawful for us to pay taxes to Caesar or not?"

Jesus saw that they were trying to trick Him. If He answered, "Yes," they could argue that He was supporting the Romans against His own people. But if He answered, "No," they could report Him to the Roman authorities as being disloyal to the government.

"Why do you test Me?" Jesus demanded. "Show Me a denarius."

The men handed Him a bright Roman coin. Jesus held it up and asked, "Whose image and inscription does it have?"

"Caesar's," they replied.

"Render therefore to Caesar the things that are Caesar's, and to God the things that are God's," Jesus told them. Quickly the men turned away, for they were amazed at His answer and could think of nothing more to say.

One day Jesus and His disciples were standing in the temple court. They watched the rich people with their servants, bringing in bags of silver and boxes of gold to the temple treasury. These rich people made a great show of giving their large offerings.

But then, while they were watching, a little woman, old and bent over, came hobbling toward the treasury box. They could see at once that she was a widow, the poorest of the poor. When she came to the collection box, she quickly dropped two small copper coins into it and turned to leave.

The Savior noticed the look of happiness on the poor woman's face, and He said to His disciples, "Truly I say to you that this poor widow has put in more than all; for all these"—He motioned to the rich people standing there with their servants—"out of their abundance have put in offerings for God, but she out of her poverty put in all the livelihood that she had."

Among the thousands of people who came to the temple for the Passover festival were some Greeks who had heard of the Mighty Prince. One day they came to Philip, one of Jesus' disciples, and said, "Sir, we wish to see Jesus."

Philip hurried to tell his friend Andrew, and the two disciples went to find Jesus. When the Master heard that men from a foreign country wanted to know about the kingdom of God, He said, "The hour has come that the Son of Man should be glorified."

He knew that the time was near when He would be arrested, tried, and condemned to die. In His human nature, Jesus wanted to avoid suffering, just as you and I would. So He prayed, "Now, My soul is troubled, and what shall I say? 'Father, save Me from this hour'? But for this purpose I came to this hour. 'Father, glorify Your name.' "

In that moment, a Voice thundered from the sky and echoed through the temple courts. The Voice said, "I have both glorified it and will glorify it again."

The crowd standing nearby heard the voice. Some said it was only thunder. Others declared, "An angel has spoken to Him."

Jesus spoke calmly to the wondering people. "This voice did not come because of Me," He told them, "but for your sake." The Master looked at the men, women, and children standing around Him, and He loved them all. He longed to save them from evil, sorrow, and suffering. He spoke to them again, "I have

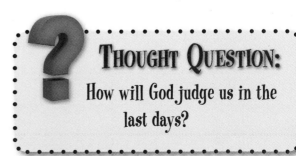

THOUGHT QUESTION: How will God judge us in the last days?

come as a light into the world, that whoever believes in Me should not abide in darkness. And if anyone hears My words and does not believe, I do not judge him; for I did not come to judge the world but to save the world. He who rejects Me, and does not receive My words, has that which judges him—the word that I have spoken will judge him in the last day. For I have not spoken on My own authority; but the Father who sent Me gave Me a command, what I should say and what I should speak. And I know that His command is everlasting life."

THE LORD'S SUPPER

Matthew 26:14–30; Mark 14:12–50; John 13:1–30

Judas Iscariot, the disciple who acted as treasurer for the Twelve, was unusually quiet during the days following the Master's triumphal entry into Jerusalem. On several occasions when Jesus and His followers appeared in the temple, Judas was absent. He was busy with his own secret plans, and even when he was with the Master, he acted strange and seemed to be uncomfortable.

The truth of the matter was that Judas had gone to the priests in their secret council and offered to betray his Master to them. Thinking only of money, he had said, "What are you willing to give me if I deliver Him to you?"

The priests whispered together, and at last they came to an agreement. They counted out thirty pieces of silver and placed them in the hand of Judas. From that time on, the betrayer waited for an opportunity to turn Jesus over to His enemies.

On Thursday afternoon, preparations were being made in every house in Jerusalem to eat the Passover supper. Thinking of this special occasion, the disciples came to the Master and asked, "Where do You want us to prepare for You to eat the Passover?"

121

"Go into the city," directed Jesus, "and a man will meet you carrying a pitcher of water; follow him. Wherever he goes in, say to the master of the house, 'The Teacher says, "Where is the guest room in which I may eat the Passover with My disciples?" ' Then he will show you a large upper room, furnished and prepared; there make ready for us."

Peter and John followed their Master's instructions and found everything as He had told them. They prepared the Passover supper of roast lamb, bread, and bitter herbs.

In the upstairs room was a table with places around it for Jesus and His disciples. Candles were burning that evening as the thirteen men entered to eat the Passover supper. Jesus was sad, for He had heard His followers arguing and muttering angry words at one another. James and John had asked Him for the highest positions in the kingdom, and the other disciples were jealous because they hadn't thought to ask first.

While the disciples bickered, Jesus arose from the table and took off His beautiful outer robe. Then He fastened a towel around His waist, took a basin of water, and knelt before the nearest disciple. He began to wash the dust from the man's feet.

All at once, there was silence. The twelve disciples were astonished. They were proud because they were disciples of the Man they believed would soon be the King of Israel. They had neglected to hire a servant to wash the dust of the road from their feet. And certainly none of the Twelve would stoop to this humble duty. But now, while they were arguing about who would

> ## GOD SAYS:
>
> "For as often as you eat this bread and drink this cup, you proclaim the Lord's death till He comes."
> —1 Corinthians 11:26

have the best positions in the coming kingdom, Jesus, the Mighty Prince, knelt before His disciples and washed their feet!

When the Master came to Simon Peter, he protested, "Lord, are You washing my feet?"

THOUGHT QUESTION: How do we celebrate the Lord's Supper today?

"What I am doing you do not understand now, but you will know after this," Jesus replied.

"You shall never wash my feet!" Peter insisted, for he knew that he should have been willing to do this humble task for the other disciples himself.

"If I do not wash you," Jesus told him, "you have no part with Me."

"Lord," Peter answered quickly, "not my feet only, but also my hands and my head!" In spite of his faults, Peter really did love Jesus dearly.

In a few moments Jesus came to Judas and washed his feet. The Master knew that this man had turned traitor. Already the thirty pieces of silver were jingling in his bag, but in spite of this, Jesus loved Judas and longed to save him for His kingdom. What a lesson of forgiveness Jesus gave to all His followers! We are to love everyone, even our enemies.

When Jesus had washed the feet of all the disciples, He came to the table and asked them, "Do you know what I have done to you? You call me Teacher and Lord, and you say well, for so I am. If I then, your Lord and Teacher, have washed your feet, you also ought to wash one another's feet. For I have given you an example, that you should do as I have done to you."

After the Passover supper, while the group was at the table, Jesus took bread and blessed it. Then He broke it in pieces and gave some to each of His disciples, saying, "Take, eat; this is My body." Next, He took a cup of wine and gave thanks and handed it to His disciples. Each one drank from it. The wine represented the blood He would soon shed on the cross.

This was the Lord's Supper. Jesus gave this special service to us as a memorial of His death and resurrection. When we take part in the service we look forward to the day when we will be with our Savior in His kingdom, for He told the disciples, "I will no longer drink of the fruit of the vine until that day when I drink it new in the kingdom of God."

QUICK FACT:

Jesus gave Judas every chance not to betray Him.

As the disciples were at the table, they saw that their Master was troubled. Finally He spoke in a solemn, almost broken, voice. "I say to you," He said hesitantly, "one of you who eats with Me will betray Me."

The disciples looked at each other, hurt and puzzled. They didn't understand what Jesus was saying. John, who was next to Jesus, turned to Him and asked, "Lord, who is it?" One by one, around the circle, the disciples murmured, "Is it I?"

Jesus answered, "It is he to whom I shall give a piece of bread when I have dipped it." Then He dipped the piece of bread in the dish, and while the twelve men waited breathlessly, He handed it to Judas Iscariot and said to him, "What you do, do quickly."

Judas arose from the table and walked out the door without a word. He went out into the night, a lost man!

BETRAYED WITH A KISS

Matthew 26:36–56; Mark 14:27–50; Luke 22:39–53;
John 13:31–38; 14; 18:1–12

Eleven faithful disciples remained with Jesus in the upper room after Judas had slipped away. To them Jesus said, "A new commandment I give to you, that you love one another; as I have loved you, that you also love one another. By this all will know that you are My disciples, if you have love for one another."

"Lord, where are You going?" Simon Peter wanted to know.

"Where I am going you cannot follow Me now, but you shall follow Me afterward," Jesus answered.

"Lord, why can I not follow You now? I will lay down my life for Your sake."

"Will you lay down your life for My sake?" Jesus replied. Then He shook his head and looked at Peter, and said, "Most assuredly, I say to you the rooster shall not crow till you have denied me three times."

Peter sat back, stunned into silence. He was sure that he would always be true to the Mighty Prince. He had been faithful since the day that Jesus had called him to leave his fishing boat. Disown the Master! Peter was sure that was the last thing on earth he would ever do. "If I have to die with You, I will not deny You!" Peter insisted. And all the disciples said the same.

126

As Jesus saw the troubled look on their faces, He spoke encouraging words to them. "Let not your heart be troubled," He said. "You believe in God, believe also in Me.

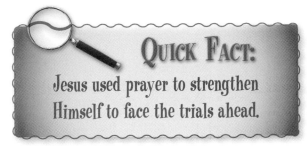

QUICK FACT:
Jesus used prayer to strengthen Himself to face the trials ahead.

In My Father's house are many mansions; if it were not so, I would have told you. I go to prepare a place for you. And if I go and prepare a place for you, I will come again and receive you to Myself; that where I am, there you may be also. And where I go you know, and the way you know."

Thomas, who always tended to doubt, said, "Lord, we do not know where You are going, and how can we know the way?"

"I am way, the truth, and the life. No one comes to the Father except through Me," Jesus answered. He was telling His disciples that He would soon be going back to His Father, but He promised to come again and take them, and us, home with Him to heaven where they would be with Him forever.

When He had finished comforting His disciples, Jesus led them out of the upstairs room. The little group made its way out of Jerusalem to the other side of Kidron Brook, where there was a beautiful garden called Gethsemane. It was a place that Judas knew well, for Jesus had gone there often with His disciples.

The night was still and cloudless. A full moon shone down upon the garden, and the trees cast long shadows across the grass. Jesus was silent; sorrow filled His face. At the entrance to the garden, He said to His disciples, "Sit here while I pray."

Then He took Peter, James, and John with Him farther into the garden. He dreaded what was soon to happen, and distress weighed heavily on Him. "My soul is exceedingly sorrowful, even to death," He told the trusted three. "Stay here and watch."

Then He went on a little farther and threw Himself on the ground. He prayed to His Father, asking that if it were possible, He might be spared from the suffering and death that lay ahead. Jesus did not want to suffer and die any more than anyone would. "Father," Jesus prayed, "all things are possible for You. Take this cup away from Me; nevertheless, not what I will, but what You will."

After a while, He came back to His three disciples and found them sound asleep! "Simon, are you sleeping?" Jesus asked Peter. "Could you not watch one hour? Watch and pray, lest you enter into temptation. The spirit indeed is willing, but the flesh is weak."

Again, Jesus went to pray, and when He returned the second time, He found the disciples still asleep. Try as they might, they couldn't keep their eyes open. A third time Jesus went alone and prayed for strength to face death. When He came back this time, He said to the disciples, "Are you still sleeping and resting? It is enough!"

Through the trees came the sound of voices and the glow of lighted torches. "Behold," Jesus said, "the Son of Man is being betrayed into the hands of sinners. Rise, let us be going. See, My betrayer is at hand."

In a moment, Jesus and the disciples were surrounded by a mob of men with swords and clubs. Judas was at their head. He had instructed the soldiers, "Whomever I kiss, He is the One; seize Him and lead Him away safely." So Judas slipped up close to Jesus and said, "Rabbi, Rabbi!" Then he kissed Jesus.

"Friend, why

have you come?" asked Jesus. "Are you betraying the Son of Man with a kiss?" Even in the moment of betrayal, Jesus called Judas a friend!

Quickly the soldiers stepped forward to tie Jesus' hands, but at that moment, Peter, who had been too frightened to move, remembered his vow to die with Jesus if need be. As the soldiers laid hold of his Master, Peter went into action. He drew his sword and started swinging it wildly at the man nearest him. Fortunately, it was Malchus, the high priest's servant, and not a Roman soldier that Peter hit, or he would probably have been killed instantly. As it was, Peter's sword grazed the man's head and sliced off his right ear.

The wounded man cried out, and Jesus turned to Peter, saying, "Put your sword into the sheath. Shall I not drink the cup which My Father has given Me?" Then the Master touched the wounded man's ear and healed it.

Turning to the priests and elders who had come to help capture Him, the Mighty Prince asked, "Have you come out, as against a robber, with swords and clubs? When I was with you daily in the temple, you did not try to seize Me. But this is your hour, and the power of darkness."

As the soldiers tied Jesus' hands and led Him away, the eleven disciples quickly disappeared in the darkness. One of the mob caught hold of the robe of a young man who was standing close by, but the frightened boy slipped out of his robe and ran away naked! So it was that in His time of greatest need all the

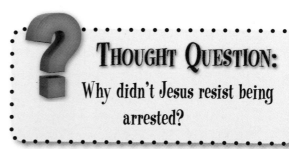

THOUGHT QUESTION: Why didn't Jesus resist being arrested?

Master's followers deserted Him; Jesus, the Mighty Prince, was alone in the hands of His enemies.

JESUS A PRISONER

Matthew 26:57–27:10; Mark 14:53–72; John 18:12–27

I t was past midnight by now, and the city of Jerusalem was asleep when the Roman soldiers hurried their Prisoner down the dark, narrow streets to the palace of Annas, the powerful man who headed the family of Jewish priests. Caiaphas, the son-in-law of Annas, was the high priest at this time. He would be the one who would lead out in the trial of Jesus, yet the elderly Annas wanted to see the Man of Nazareth who had stirred the nation by His teachings and by His deeds of love. So Jesus was brought first to Annas.

The hall was lighted by smoking torches when Jesus entered and stood before this crafty politician. The Master read Annas's purposes like an open book. He saw a man who cared little for the people. At heart, Annas was a greedy, grasping tyrant who was interested only in power.

Jesus knew that Annas was trying to take His life, so when the priest questioned Him about His disciples and His teachings, the Master answered, "I spoke openly to the world. I always taught in synagogues and in the temple, where the Jews always meet, and in secret I have said nothing. Why do you ask Me? Ask those who have heard Me what I said to them. Indeed they know what I said."

Annas was afraid that Jesus would reveal the wickedness in his heart, so he didn't say anything more to Jesus. Instead, he commanded the soldiers to take the Prisoner to Caiaphas, his son-in-law. But he hadn't lost his hatred for the Mighty Prince, and he would continue to use every means possible to destroy Him.

It wasn't far from the house of Annas to the palace of Caiaphas, and the soldiers hurried their Prisoner through the deserted streets. In the early hours of the morning, Jesus entered the judgment hall where the members of the Sanhedrin, the Jewish court, were assembling.

The Savior was not given a fair trial; everything that took place during these hours was illegal. A mob had been hired to shout out and demand His death. Witnesses had been paid to tell false stories about Him. And the Jewish leaders were afraid to permit the trial to take place in the light of day, for Jesus had many friends in Jerusalem who would rise up against the unjust trial. So, the members of the council assembled secretly and hurriedly in the judgment hall.

Caiaphas, the high priest, took his seat on the platform. He looked down at Jesus. The Master, calm and humble, stood before the high priest with bound hands, surrounded by a guard of burly Roman soldiers. As he looked at Jesus, even Caiaphas felt his heart being touched. He knew this Man was not guilty of the things He was accused of. But the high priest quickly brushed the truth aside and ordered the trial to begin.

The council tried to find evidence against Jesus that they could use to sentence Him to death. They called their witnesses. One

GOD SAYS:
"He was oppressed and He was afflicted, Yet He opened not His mouth."
-Isaiah 53:7

testified, "We heard Him say, 'I will destroy this temple made with hands, and within three days I will build another made without hands.' " But when they called another witness, he disagreed with what the first witness had said. There was confusion and uproar in the council chamber. It was becoming clear that the witnesses were making up their testimony and couldn't keep their stories straight.

Caiaphas stood up and stepped down from the platform to stand before the Prisoner. "Do You answer nothing?" he demanded. "What is it these men testify against You?"

The Son of God looked straight into the eyes of the high priest, but He said not a word.

In fury, Caiaphas ordered, "I put You under oath by the living God: Tell us if You are the Christ, the Son of God!"

For a moment the great hall was deathly silent. The scribes held their pens in midair, awaiting the answer the Prisoner must give under oath. All eyes were focused upon Jesus.

"It is as you said," the Master answered quietly. "Nevertheless, I say to you, hereafter you will see the Son of Man sitting at the right hand of the Power, and coming on the clouds of heaven."

The high priest shrank back before the penetrating eyes of Jesus, and the members of the council were startled and afraid. Then, seizing his robe, Caiaphas tore it from top to bottom to show that he was horrified at Jesus' claim to be the Messiah. He shouted, "He has spoken blasphemy! What farther need do we have of witnesses? Look, now you have heard His blasphemy! What do you think?"

From every corner of the judgment hall came the cry of the priests and scribes and leaders: "He is deserving of death." As the court adjourned, Jesus was taken into the guardroom by the soldiers, and there the mob surrounded Him. They spit in His face, they blindfolded Him and struck Him on the head.

Then they taunted Him, saying, "Prophesy to us, Christ! Who is the one who struck You?"

Before the high priest and elders left the judgment hall, a wild-eyed man came running up. He had listened to the trial and heard the sentence pronounced by the Jewish court. This man stood terrified in front of Caiaphas, the high priest. Opening a money bag, he threw thirty pieces of silver down on the pavement in front of the priests and elders.

The coins clattered on the stones, and some rolled off into dark corners of the room, but no one moved to pick them up. The leaders watched in amazement as Judas Iscariot, the disciple who had betrayed his Lord, fell sobbing before Caiaphas and cried out, "I have sinned by betraying innocent blood."

"What is that to us?" Caiaphas said scornfully. "You see to it!"

Looking at the silver on the floor and then into the hard faces of the rulers, Judas got to his feet and rushed out of the hall. Taking a piece of rope, he went to an open field. He threw the rope over the limb of a tree, tied one end around his neck, and then hanged himself. This is how the traitor died—the disciple who had sold his Master for a few silver coins.

QUICK FACT:
Jesus could have destroyed His accusers at any time.

Meanwhile, another disciple had been sitting in the courtyard outside the judgment hall, trying to listen to all that was going on inside. Simon Peter stood by a small fire, warming himself. The warmth felt good, for cold chills of fear were running up and down his spine. Peter was afraid, not only for his Master, but for himself. Roman soldiers stood only a few feet away. If they knew that he was one of Jesus' disciples, they might arrest him and put him on trial as well!

While he stood listening to the trial, a young woman came up to him. The firelight was shining on Peter's face. The woman looked at Peter and said, "You also were with Jesus of Galilee."

Peter stiffened, but his face betrayed no emotion. "I do not know what you are saying," he replied, shaking his head. A few minutes later, he slipped away from the group around the fire and went to stand near the gate. There, another young woman saw him and said to those standing nearby, "This fellow also was with Jesus of Nazareth."

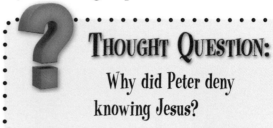

THOUGHT QUESTION: Why did Peter deny knowing Jesus?

"I do not know the Man!" insisted Peter roughly, and this time he added a curse word to sound convincing. The people looked at him curiously. One of them came over a little later and said, "Surely you also are one of them, for your speech betrays you."

Sweat broke out on Peter's forehead, and, in a fury of fright, he began swearing and cursing, using the strongest language he knew. "I do not know the Man!" he shouted.

There was a moment of jeering laughter that echoed in the dark courtyard, and soon the men turned away to other excitement. In the silence that followed, Peter heard a rooster crow on the wall above him, and immediately the words of his Master came back to him, "Before the rooster crows, you will deny Me three times."

Peter bowed his head as tears came to his eyes. Just at that moment, the soldiers marched Jesus from the judgment hall, and through his tears Peter caught a glimpse of his Master. In that same instant, Jesus turned and looked at Peter. It was a look of love and sympathy. Peter could stand it no longer. Heartbroken, he turned and ran from the courtyard—out into the dark, silent streets and wept bitterly.

THE KING OF THE JEWS

Matthew 27:11–31; Luke 23:1–25; John 18:28–40

It was early Friday morning when the soldiers led the Prisoner into the hall of Pontius Pilate, the Roman governor of Judea. Pilate was especially cautious during this time when the Jewish festivals were taking place, because thousands of visitors were in Jerusalem from all over Israel and any kind of disturbance could cause rioting or some other upheaval that would quickly come to the ears of the emperor in Rome.

As soon as Pilate saw the members of the Sanhedrin file into his judgment hall with their Prisoner, he realized that this was an unusual case. When all was quiet, he asked the Jews what the charge was against this Man, this Jesus of Nazareth.

"We found this fellow perverting the nation, and forbidding to pay taxes to Caesar, saying that He Himself is Christ, a King," the Jewish rulers falsely charged.

The Roman ruler looked carefully at the Prisoner. He had dealt with all kinds of criminals, but never before had he seen a person who looked so kind and noble. Pilate saw no sign of guilt or fear in the Prisoner's face. He wondered who Jesus was and the real reason the Jewish leaders had brought Him to his judgment hall. Then, turning to Jesus, he asked, "Are You the King of the Jews?"

"It is as you say," replied Jesus.

This statement didn't worry Pilate, for he had the power of Rome behind him. If this Man believed that He was a leader of the Jews, let Him think so. Pilate was certain that this Jesus would get nowhere against the mighty armies of the emperor. With careless indifference Pilate turned to the Jewish rulers and said, "I find no fault in this Man."

In desperation, the priests assured Pilate, "He stirs up the people, teaching throughout all Judea, beginning from Galilee to this place." They added, "If He were not an evildoer, we would not have delivered Him up to you."

"You take Him and judge Him according to your law," Pilate told them, impatient with their quibbling.

"It is not lawful for us to put anyone to death," they whined.

Pilate had heard them say that Jesus had caused trouble from Galilee to Jerusalem. And this gave him a way out of having to deal with the situation. Herod, the ruler of Galilee, was in Jerusalem at this time. Why not send this Man from Galilee to the ruler of that territory and let him decide the case? So Pilate sent the Jewish rulers and their Prisoner to Herod.

Herod was delighted to see Jesus. He had wanted to talk to this Man for a long time, and now that Jesus was here, Herod hoped that He would perform some miracle for him. For some time, Herod questioned Jesus, but He answered nothing—not one word. Finally, the ruler of Galilee and his Roman guards poked fun at Jesus. They took a royal robe with gold fringe and put it around His shoulders. They mocked Him and called Him "King of the Jews." But when they grew tired of their sport at last, they sent Jesus and the Jewish rulers back to Pilate to determine His fate.

> **GOD SAYS:**
>
> "Christ also suffered for us, leaving us an example, that you should follow His steps." -1 Peter 2: 21

When Jesus again stood before the Roman governor, Pilate said to the priests and leaders of the Jewish council, "You have brought this Man to me, as one who misleads the people. And indeed, having examined Him in your presence, I have found no fault in this Man concerning those things of which you accuse Him; no neither did Herod . . . and indeed nothing deserving of death has been done by Him. I will therefore chastise Him and release Him."

At this, the mob, which was in the pay of the Jewish rulers, began to shout, "Away with this Man, and release to us Barabbas."

Barabbas was a well-known prisoner who had committed murder and other violent crimes deserving of death. It was the custom for the Roman governor to release a prisoner to the people at the time of the Passover festival. When the crowd shouted to him to release Barabbas, Pilate asked the Jewish leaders and the crowd, "Which of the two do you want me to release to you?"

Again the mob shouted, "Barabbas!"

"What then shall I do with Jesus who is called Christ?" asked the Roman ruler.

"Let Him be crucified!" came the cry of the mob.

At this moment, while Pilate sat on his throne, he received a message from his wife. With a frown on his forehead, Pilate read her words. "Have nothing to do with that just Man, for I have suffered many things today in a dream because of Him."

A dream! This Man seemed to have a strange and wonderful power. Pilate pondered what he should do. Should he take the counsel of his wife and her dream? No, that would be weak; he would make his own decision.

Pilate called Jesus into his private room and asked, "Are You the King of the Jews?"

"Are you speaking for yourself about this, or did others tell you this concerning Me?" asked the Mighty Prince.

Pilate replied, "Am I a Jew? Your own nation and the chief priests have delivered You to me. What have You done?"

"My kingdom is not of this world," Jesus said. "If My kingdom were of this world, My servants would fight, so that I should not be delivered to the Jews; but now My kingdom is not from here."

QUICK FACT:
There was something in Jesus that held Pilate back from signing his death warrant.

"Are You a king then?" Pilate asked Him.

"You say rightly that I am a king," replied the Mighty Prince. "For this cause I was born, and for this cause I have come into the world, that I should bear witness to the truth. Everyone who is of the truth hears My voice."

Pilate felt drawn by these wonderful words, but he bit his lip and scornfully answered, "What is truth?" Then without another word he went outside and faced the Jews.

"I find no fault in Him at all," he announced. "But you have a custom that I should release someone to you at the Passover. Do you therefore want me to release to you the King of the Jews?"

"Not this Man, but Barabbas!" the crowd insisted.

The Roman ruler took Jesus and had Him whipped before the crowd. The soldiers put an old purple robe around Christ's shoulders and a crown of thorns on His head.

"Behold, I am bringing Him out to you, that you may know that I find no fault in Him," cried Pilate, presenting Jesus once more to the crowd.

"Crucify Him, crucify Him," the frenzied mob shouted louder than ever.

When Pilate saw that he was gaining nothing, but that a riot was about to start, he took some water and washed his hands in the presence of the crowd, saying. "I am innocent of the blood of this just Person. You see to it." But no matter what he said, Pilate *was* guilty, and no water could ever wash the stain of sin from his bloody hands.

Then all the people answered, "His blood be on us and on our children."

Then Pilate ordered the soldiers to unchain the vile criminal Barabbas and set him free. But the brutal Roman soldiers took Jesus into their barracks and tortured Him. They took a Roman whip, which had sharp bits of metal and bone at the end of each cord, and struck Him forty times on the back. The whip tore His skin into strips, and the blood poured out. Many prisoners died from such a horrible beating.

THOUGHT QUESTION:
Why didn't Pilate let Jesus go when he knew Jesus was innocent?

Then the soldiers stripped off Jesus' clothes and put an old robe over His shoulders. They pushed a crown of wild thorns down on His forehead until the blood oozed out. They put a stick in His hand and knelt before Him in mockery, saying, "Hail, King of the Jews!"

They spit on Him and struck Him on the head with the stick. During all the sneering, torment, and the torture Jesus answered not a word. His heart of love went out to everyone, even to these soldiers who were tormenting Him.

When the soldiers had finished their fiendish torture, they led the Mighty Prince away to Golgotha to be crucified.

NAILED TO THE CROSS

Matthew 27:32–56; Mark 15:21–41; Luke 23:26–56; John 19:17–42

Jesus' back was bloody and torn from the beating He had received, and He had been without sleep or rest for many hours. But the Roman soldiers forced Him to carry the heavy wooden cross along the way that led toward Golgotha. It was their custom that prisoners who were going to be crucified had to carry the heavy cross to the place of execution. Then bystanders would know the horrible death He was about to suffer.

On that Friday morning, Jesus carried His cross through the streets of Jerusalem. Two other men had been sentenced to be crucified with Him, and they, too, were carrying their crosses. The suffering and the agony became too great for the Savior. He staggered and fell under the weight of the cross. The Roman soldiers saw that their Prisoner was too weak to carry the cross any farther, and they wondered where they could find someone who would carry the humiliating symbol.

A man named Simon, a Cyrenian, was coming into the city at this time. He heard the taunts and jeers of the crowd surrounding the prisoners, and he watched the tragic scene with amazement. When the soldiers saw this stranger, they quickly grabbed him and forced him to carry Jesus' cross.

When they came at last to the place called Golgotha, or Calvary, they offered Jesus a drink of wine to help deaden His pain, but He would not drink it. Then the soldier laid the three crosses on the ground and dug holes in which to set the heavy timbers. The sky was dark and threatening, and it seemed as if a storm were gathering.

The soldiers placed the two robbers on their crosses and held them down while they nailed their hands and feet to the wooden beams. Then the soldiers stretched Jesus upon His cross and nailed His hands and feet to it with great spikes. Then the crosses were lifted toward the sky and dropped into holes in the ground.

Through all of this agony Jesus made no murmur or complaint. His face remained calm, but great drops of sweat stood on His brow.

> **GOD SAYS:**
> " 'Let all the house of Israel know assuredly that God has made this Jesus, whom you crucified, both Lord and Christ.' " –Acts 2:36

There was no one standing by to offer a word of sympathy, no one to wipe His forehead or to comfort Him. Yet, while His enemies worked, Jesus prayed, "Father, forgive them, for they do not know what they do."

Pilate, the Roman ruler, had a sign placed upon Jesus' cross. It read,

"JESUS OF NAZARETH,
THE KING OF THE JEWS"

By this time hundreds of people in the city had heard that Jesus had been arrested and sentenced to be crucified. They came out to Golgotha to watch the Teacher die. The crowd jeered at Him, wagging their heads and saying, "You who destroy the temple and build it in three days, save Yourself! If You are the Son of God, come down from the cross."

The priests and Jewish leaders also stood there, gloating in their triumph. "He saved others; Himself He cannot save," they said mockingly. "If He is the King of Israel, let Him now come down from the cross, and we will believe Him. He trusted in God; let Him deliver Him now if He will have Him; for He said, 'I am the Son of God.' "

At noon the sky became black, and the people standing around the cross began looking at each other anxiously. Was something terrible about to happen?

When the soldiers had crucified Jesus, they took His clothes and divided them into four piles, one for each of them. Now, Jesus' robe was woven without a seam, in one piece from top to bottom. The soldiers said, "Let us not tear it, but cast lots for it, whose it shall be."

One of the robbers hanging on the cross beside Jesus said, "If You are the Christ, save Yourself and us."

But the other robber reproved his evil companion, saying, "Do you not even fear God, seeing you are under the same condemnation? And we

indeed justly, for we receive the due reward of our deeds; but this Man has done nothing wrong." Then, looking at Jesus, the dying Son of God, the robber said, "Lord, remember me when You come into Your kingdom."

In that hour when darkness covered the earth and human beings were rejecting the Savior of the world, Jesus promised eternal life to the thief on the cross who had faith in the Mighty Prince and in His power to save.

Near the cross stood Mary, Jesus' mother, along with two other women. When Jesus saw His mother and John the disciple whom He loved, He said to His mother, "Woman, behold your son!" Then turning His head toward John, He said, "Behold your mother!" Jesus meant that John was to take care of His mother, Mary. And from that time John took Jesus' mother into his home and supported her like a son.

During His hours of suffering on the cross, Jesus longed for a drink of water. "I thirst!" He called out. One of the soldiers soaked a sponge in sour wine and held it to the Savior's lips. Then Jesus cried out, "It is finished!" and He bowed His head and died. The work of the Mighty Prince, the Messiah, the Lamb of God, as predicted by the prophets, was completed. Jesus had died to save human beings from eternal death, the wages of sin.

QUICK FACT:
Jesus chose to suffer and die so that we might have a chance at eternal life.

After Jesus died, the Roman captain who had watched the crucifixion said, "Certainly this was a righteous Man!" And he added, "Truly, this Man was the Son of God!"

When Jesus died there was a violent earthquake. People who were standing around the cross were thrown to the ground.

Priests and leaders, soldiers and bystanders, cringed in fear at the earthquake's roar. They knew that they had crucified an in-nocent Man and that their hearts would never again be at peace.

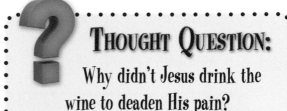

THOUGHT QUESTION:
Why didn't Jesus drink the wine to deaden His pain?

The priests in the Holy Place of the temple were amazed and frightened at the strange thing that happened there when Je-sus died. The beautiful curtain that separated the Holy Place from the Most Holy Place in the temple was torn apart from top to bottom. It was a sign that the sacrifice of lambs no longer meant anything, because Jesus, the Lamb of God, had died.

It was near sundown, and the bodies could not be left hang-ing on the crosses over the Sabbath. To make sure Jesus was dead, one of the Roman soldiers pierced His side, and blood and water came out.

Soon after this, Joseph, a rich man from Arimathaea, who had been a secret disciple of Jesus, went to Pilate and asked him for the Savior's body. The Roman ruler ordered that it be given to Joseph, and the rich man took down Jesus' body from the cross. Nicodemus, a ruler of the Jews who had once come se-cretly at night to talk with Jesus, now boldly came forward as a follower of the Master. He helped Joseph prepare Jesus' body for burial. They wrapped it with spices in long strips of clean linen cloth.

There was a garden near the place where Jesus had been cruci-fied, and in that garden was a new tomb that had been carved out of the solid rock. The tomb belonged to Joseph, and no one had ever been buried in it. It was almost sundown, and the Sabbath was coming when they placed Jesus' body in Joseph's new tomb.

The Jewish leaders went to Pilate and said, "Sir, we remember, while He was still alive, how that deceiver said, 'After three days I will rise.' Therefore command that the tomb be made secure until the third day, lest His disciples come by night and steal Him away, and say to the people, 'He has risen from the dead.' So the last deception will be worse than the first."

"You have a guard," Pilate told them. "Go your way, make it as secure as you know how."

Then the guard of Roman soldiers went out to the tomb in the garden and put the Roman seal on the stone that covered the entrance. This meant that anyone who tried to break the seal and move the stone would be punished with death.

The disciples spent the Sabbath mourning for their lost Master. They were near despair, for all their hopes had turned to ashes.

THE EMPTY TOMB

Mark 16:1–20; Luke 24:1–34; John 20

Early Sunday morning, after the holy Sabbath day had ended, several women—Mary, the mother of Jesus, Mary of Magdala, and Salome—made their way to the tomb where Jesus' body had been buried. They wanted to finish preparing His body for burial with more sweet spices and ointments. As they made their way along the dark, lonely road they said, "Who will roll away the stone from the door of the tomb for us?"

When they arrived at the tomb, they found things very different from what they had expected. They didn't know that an angel had already come from heaven and had rolled back the great stone. At this, the Roman soldiers on guard had trembled with fear and fallen down like dead men.

Now, as the women came to the tomb, they saw the angel sitting upon the stone. He was dressed in clothes as white as snow. He said to them, "Do not be alarmed. You seek Jesus of Nazareth, who was crucified. He is risen! He is not here. See the place where they laid Him."

> **GOD SAYS:**
> " 'They will scourge Him and kill Him. And the third day He will rise again.' "
> –Luke 18:33

The amazed women looked into the empty tomb. They didn't know what to do. It was all too wonderful for words! Then the angel said, "Go, tell His disciples—and Peter—that He is going before you into Galilee; there you will see Him, as He said to you."

Mary of Magdala could not believe what she had heard. She ran back to the city and found Peter and John, and said to them, "They have taken away the Lord out of the tomb, and we do not know where they have laid Him."

When Peter and John heard these words they started running to the tomb. John was younger, and he outran Peter and reached the tomb first. He saw the linen cloths lying on the ground, but he did not go inside the tomb. When Peter arrived he went inside and saw the cloths and also the folded handkerchief that had covered Jesus' face—but there was no body in the tomb.

Peter and John were amazed, but they, too, couldn't believe that their Master had really risen from the dead and was alive again. So they went back to Jerusalem. Mary remained in the garden, however, and, as she stood there crying, two angels asked her, "Why are you weeping?"

"Because they have taken away my Lord," she replied, "and I do not know where they have laid Him." Even as she was speaking, she turned around and saw a man. It was Jesus, but she didn't recognize Him. She thought he must be someone in charge of the garden.

"Why are you weeping?" Jesus asked her. "Whom are you seeking?"

Mary still didn't realize it was Jesus. "Sir," she said to Him, "if You have carried Him away, tell me where You have laid Him, and I will take Him away."

"Mary!" said Jesus.

And all at once Mary recognized Jesus by the sound of His voice. "Rabboni!" she exclaimed. And she started to reach out to touch Him.

"Do not cling to Me," Jesus told her, "for I have not yet ascended to My Father; but go to My brethren and say to them, 'I am ascending to My Father and your Father, and to My God and your God.'"

Mary tore herself away from Jesus and hurried back into Jerusalem. She told the disciples that she had actually seen the Master with her own eyes, and she told them everything Jesus had said to her.

That same afternoon, two followers of Jesus, who had been in Jerusalem when He was crucified, were walking along the steep road that led from Jerusalem to the town of Emmaus. Their voices were low, and they were sad as they talked about the trial, crucifixion, and death of their Master. On the road, they met a Man who asked them, "What kind of conversation is this that you have with one another as you walk and are sad?"

QUICK FACT: Mary, a woman, was the first person to see Jesus after He rose from the dead.

The two followers of Jesus stopped and looked at the Man. "Are You the only stranger in Jerusalem, and have You not known the things which happened there in these days?" they asked in surprise.

"What things?" He asked.

"The things concerning Jesus of Nazareth, who was a Prophet mighty in deed and word before God and all the people, and how the chief priests and our rulers delivered Him to be condemned to death, and crucified Him. But we were hoping that it was He who was going to redeem Israel."

The Man listened intently, and the disciples went on explaining, "Indeed, besides all this, today is the third day since these things happened. Yes, and certain women of our company, who arrived at the tomb early, astonished us. When they did not find His body, they came saying that

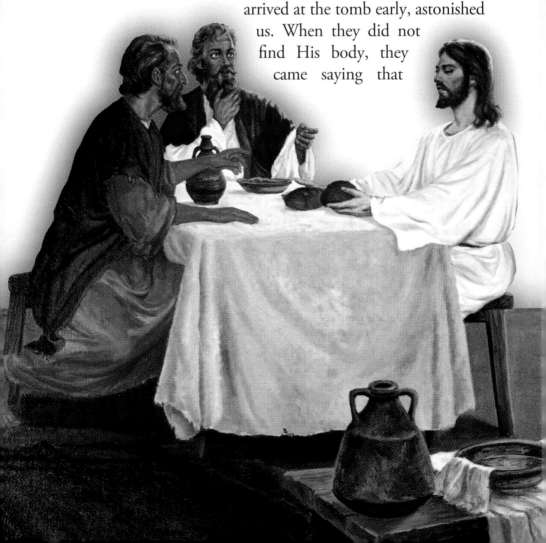

they had also seen a vision of angels who said He was alive. And certain of those who were with us went to the tomb and found it just as the women had said; but Him they did not see."

"O foolish ones," the Man exclaimed, "and slow of heart to believe in all that the prophets have spoken! Ought not the Christ to have suffered these things and to enter into His glory?"

Then, as they walked along the road, the Stranger began explaining to them all that the Scriptures had to say about the Messiah—starting with the writings of Moses and continuing through all the books of the prophets.

When they reached the village of Emmaus, the Man seemed as if He were going to continue his journey, but these two followers of Jesus wanted to hear more from Him.

"Abide with us," they urged. "for it is toward evening, and the day is far spent."

So the Man went with them, and when they sat down at the table to eat, He took some bread and blessed it and broke it in pieces and handed it to them. He did it just the way they had seen Jesus do so many times before. All at once, the eyes of the two men were opened, and they realized that the Stranger was none other than Jesus Himself!

But He immediately vanished from in front of their eyes. They looked at each other in amazement and said, "Did not our heart burn within us while He talked with us on the road, and while He opened the Scriptures to us?"

The two men hurried right back to Jerusalem. They found the other disciples and told them what had happened on the road and how Jesus had broken bread at their table.

That same evening the disciples were gathered in a house, behind locked doors, because they were afraid the Jews would come and arrest them next. They still did not believe that Jesus had actually risen from the dead.

While they were hiding there, Jesus appeared in the locked

room and stood among them. "Peace to you," He said.

They were terrified and thought He was a ghost. But Jesus showed them His hands, scarred from the nails, and His side, slashed by the soldier's spear. At last the disciples believed that it really was Jesus. They were so happy to see their Master!

"As the Father has sent Me, I also send You," Jesus told them.

Thomas, one of the twelve disciples, was not with the group in the house when Jesus appeared to them. When the rest of the disciples told him that they had seen the Master, Thomas was hurt and a little jealous that he hadn't been there too. So he said, "Unless I see in His hands the print of the nails, and put my finger into the print of the nails, and put my hand into His side, I will not believe."

THOUGHT QUESTION:
Why didn't Jesus' followers recognize Him when they first saw Him?

About a week later, the disciples were again in the house, behind locked doors. Once more Jesus came and stood among them. This time Thomas was there.

Jesus turned to Thomas and said, "Reach your finger here, and look at My hands; and reach your hand here, and put it into My side. Do not be unbelieving, but believing."

Thomas was ashamed. He knelt before Jesus and said, "My Lord and my God!"

"Thomas, because you have seen Me, you have believed," Jesus said. "Blessed are those who have not seen and yet have believed." In that moment Jesus thought of all of His followers who would live from that day to the present. We can believe in Jesus, although we haven't seen Him. He blesses us today, just as He blessed His disciples so long ago.

"I AM WITH YOU ALWAYS"

Matthew 28:11–20; John 21; Acts 1:1–12

S trange rumors were floating all around Jerusalem after Jesus came out of the grave. The Roman guards, who had been at Jesus' tomb, went into the city, after they recovered from seeing the angel, and told the priests everything that had happened. The priests bribed the soldiers with a large sum of money to say that Jesus' disciples had stolen His body at night.

A few days after Jesus' resurrection, the disciples returned to their homes in Galilee; they remembered that Jesus had said He would meet them there. They were restless without their Master to inspire and guide them. One day, as they were talking, Peter couldn't stand the idleness any longer. "I am going fishing," he declared.

"We are going with you also," the other disciples said, glad to have something to do.

It was getting dark, and night was the best time to fish, so they climbed into a fishing boat and rowed out into the lake. All night long, they kept lowering their nets into the water, but they didn't catch a single fish. As the first streaks of light were dawning over the eastern hills, the disciples gave up and began rowing their boat ashore. As they came near land, a Man on the beach called out to them. "Have you any food?" He asked.

"No," came an echoing voice across the water.

"Cast the net on the right side of the boat, and you will find some," the Man told them.

The disciples did what the Man said, and a few minutes later their net was so full of fish and so heavy they couldn't pull it back into the boat! John realized who the Man on the beach must be. "It is the Lord!" he said to Peter.

When Peter heard that, he jumped into the water and began swimming for shore as fast as he could! It wasn't very far away. The other disciples, however, came to shore in the boat, dragging the heavy net behind them. At last they were able to bring in the catch of fish. They were tired and hungry from fishing all night. Jesus had a fire burning on the shore; there were fish cooking on the coals and bread enough for everyone.

"Bring some of the fish which you have just caught," Jesus said. So Peter pulled the net up on the shore and counted the catch. There were 153 large fish.

Peter and the others became so interested in counting the catch that they forgot about breakfast. Suddenly they heard Jesus call, "Come and eat breakfast." When the men sat down around the fire, Jesus handed bread and fish to each one, and they all ate as much as they wanted.

When breakfast was over, Jesus said to Peter, "Simon, son of Jonah, do you love Me more than these?"

"Yes, Lord," replied Peter. "You know that I love You."

"Feed My lambs," said Jesus.

A second time Jesus asked, "Simon, son of Jonah, do you love Me?"

"Yes, Lord," Peter answered once more. "You know that I love You."

"Tend My sheep," said Jesus.

A third time Jesus turned to Peter and asked, "Simon, son of Jonah, do you love Me?"

QUICK FACT:

Jesus wanted the other disciples to see Peter was truly sorry for denying Him.

Peter was hurt because Jesus had asked him three times if he loved Him. "Lord," he replied humbly, "You know all things; You know that I love You."

"Feed My sheep," said Jesus.

In this way, Jesus kindly reminded Peter that he had denied his Master three times just before the crucifixion. Peter realized what Jesus was doing. He had learned his lesson. He would never deny the Mighty Prince again.

Jesus lived on earth for almost six weeks after He rose from the grave. He appeared to His disciples on different occasions, and He gave them much evidence that He was indeed the risen Savior.

One day Jesus called His disciples to meet Him on a mountain in Galilee. Not only were the eleven disciples there, about five hundred other believers as well, who came because they were eager to learn about the risen Christ. The eleven disciples went from group to group, telling everyone about what they had seen and heard since the Master had been crucified. They reminded the believers of what the prophecies had said about the death and resurrection of the Messiah.

THOUGHT QUESTION:

Why was it important for Jesus to spend time on earth after His resurrection and not just go right back to heaven?

Suddenly, Jesus stood among them! Many people in the group had not seen the Mighty Prince since His death, but now they saw the marks of the nails in His hands and His feet, and they worshiped Him.

Jesus described the great task of giving the message about His love and salvation to all the world. He told His followers that He would soon leave them to return to His Father. The work that He had been doing would now have to be carried out by His followers. He gave them their assignment in these words:

> "All authority has been given to Me in heaven and on earth. Go therefore and make disciples of all the nations, baptizing them in the name of the Father and of the Son and of the Holy Spirit, teaching them to observe all things that I have commanded you; and lo, I am with you always, even to the end of the age."

After this, Jesus and His eleven disciples returned to Jerusalem. Soon the day came when the Master had to say Goodbye. The little group—Jesus and His eleven faithful disciples—left the city of Jerusalem and went out past the village of Bethany. They climbed the Mount of Olives where Jesus had spent many hours teaching these men. Near this spot He had enjoyed visiting with Lazarus, Mary, and Martha. The Garden of Gethsemane was nearby, where He had prayed and suffered on the last night before His death. Now He was about to leave these men whom He loved.

"You shall be witnesses to Me," He told them. Then He stretched out His hands to bless them. As He did so, He began to rise into the air. The disciples watched in amazement as He continued upward, higher and higher. They strained their eyes as He grew smaller for one last glimpse of the Mighty Prince. At last, a glorious cloud hid Him from their sight, but they remembered His words, "I am with you always."

Then, while the disciples were still looking up into the sky, they heard a voice. They turned and saw two angels who looked like young men dressed in white clothes. The angels said, "Men of Galilee, why do you stand gazing up into heaven? This same Jesus, who was taken up from you into heaven, will so come in like manner as you saw Him go into heaven."

Then the angels left, but their words echoed on in the disciples' minds. This same Jesus would come again! They would see Him again! Eagerly they began to plan how they would tell others about the love of Jesus. They would start in Jerusalem. Then they would go to Judea, to Samaria, and then all over the whole world.

Yes, everyone everywhere must hear the good news about Jesus—

GOD SAYS:

" 'I am with you always, even to the end of the age.' " -Matthew 28:20

His love, salvation, life, death, and resurrection. The Mighty Prince is coming again! The disciples would meet Him again face to face! And we, too, if we are faithful, will see the Mighty Prince in all His glory.

The disciples who lived with Jesus told His story and wrote it in the Gospels, but as John ended his story he wrote, "There are also many other things that Jesus did, which if they were written one by one, I suppose that even the world itself could not contain the books that would be written."

This same Mighty Prince lives in heaven today. He loves you and me—and best of all, He is coming again!